D1084067

THE

CATER-

EVOLVE, EVOLVE AGAIN,

PILLAR'S

AND THRIVE IN BUSINESS

EDGE

Sid Mohasseb

All Rights Reserved
Published in the United States by Rugged Land
9 Barrow Street, Sixth Floor, New York, NY 10014
www.ruggedland.com

Rugged Land and Colophon are Trademarks of Rugged Land, Inc.

Library of Congress Cataloging-in-Publication Data
Mohasseb, Sid
The Caterpillar's Edge:
Evolve, Evolve Again, and Thrive in Business / Sid Mohasseb
1. Business and Economics. 2.Strategic Planning.
3. Management. 4. Information Management
BUS063000

ISBN 978-0-9966363-1-5

Printed in China

Book cover, graphics, and design by:
HSU & ASSOCIATES

First Edition

*To my wife,
my true north.*

CONTENTS

PART ONE

HOPES AND FEARS:
PAST AND FUTURE

Don't cry, Caterpillar
Caterpillar, don't cry
You'll be a butterfly—by and by.
Caterpillar, please
Don't worry about a thing
"But," said Caterpillar,
"Will I still know myself—in wings?"

—Grace Nichols

CHAPTER 1
THE ADDICTION

Addiction is the irrational pursuit of a likely harmful reward. There are two common properties to addictive temptations. First, they are reinforcing (i.e., position us to want more) and second, they are rewarding (i.e., induce comfort and pleasure). Many large and small companies and their leaders are stuck in their approach to planning and execution. Some are compulsive about rigid budgeting cycles, some are obsessed with existing business models, while others are focused on defending their turf. They are guided by old habits formed in an era when competition was more static. They are, by definition, addicted and pursuing a dangerous prize.

"We are addicted to our thoughts. We cannot change anything if we cannot change our thinking."

—Dr. Santosh Kalwar, Scientist and Author

Change your thinking and you can change your future.

THE
INDISCRIMINATING DISEASE

About one in a thousand start-ups looking for capital find it, and of those, a significant number fade away quickly. While a few start-ups make it as "unicorns" (early stage companies valued at over a billion dollars), thousands waste investors' capital every year. Roughly $25 billion of venture capital money is put to work annually (less than 0.2% of U.S. GDP). This funding has influenced about 11% of private sector jobs and created companies that account for almost one-fifth of the value of the U.S. economy. Surprisingly, however, over the past decade the investor return on venture-backed companies has been close to half of the returns for the S&P 500.

Research shows that just shy of 70% of the time investors did not achieve sufficient returns to justify their investment and close to 40% of venture-backed companies returned nothing to investors. That means only one in twenty investments results in meaningful returns. There is a difference between losers and winners, and clearly, it is not how much money they raised! The winners approach the market, their business, and their competition with a different, more dynamic way of thinking and doing.

At the other extreme, many industry giants ("dinosaurs"), are reluctantly stepping aside to make room for the new generation of Wall Street darlings. Only 15% (74) of the original S&P 500 companies created in 1957 are still on the list; of those, only 2% (12) are outperforming the S&P index. In the last 30 years, the average tenure of an S&P 500 company CEO has dropped from about 10 years to 6. The average period a company remains on the S&P index is now about 14 years, half what it was 30 years ago. In other words, something is not working with the way large companies compete and evolve.

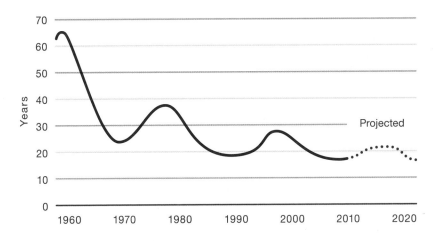

Looking ahead, a 2015 *Harvard Business Review* article reveals a dangerous trend: "We investigated the longevity of more than 30,000 public firms in the United States over a 50-year span. The results were stark: Businesses are disappearing faster than ever before. Public companies have a one in three chance of being delisted in the next five years. ... That's six times the delisting rate of companies 40 years ago." The article offers three contributing trends: i) businesses face more diverse environments, which are often harsher and less predictable; ii) technological innovation has increased the pace and impact of change—products and business models become obsolete more quickly and; iii) businesses are more interrelated than ever before—connections that can create tremendous vitality in the economy, but also increase risk.

Losers fail to recognize the less predictable competitive forces, neglect to embrace the increasing pace of change, and ignore the dynamics of a more connected world. As Einstein put it, "We cannot solve our problems with the same thinking we used to create them." Our addictions to past ways of thinking and doing can be fatal!

The losers, be they start-ups or global giants, have one thing in common—they are trapped in rituals; they fight the competitive battle with obsolete rules and tools. Failure is rooted in this approach. While every industry from retail to transportation to entertainment to health care has fundamentally changed, the way we strategize to win in the marketplace has, by and large, remained the same. This disease, which is our addiction to orthodoxies, does not discriminate based on industry, size, or age of the organization. The losers are comfortable with their old ways and ignore the likely consequences. Many start-ups think that money alone overcomes the challenges offered by a fast and furious competitive world, while many conglomerates want to address tomorrow's contests with yesterday's solutions. ***The winners see the light, kick the*** *habit, and end the cycle of sameness; they break the rigidity of their thinking and doing.*

"We can easily forgive a child who is afraid of the dark;
the real tragedy of life is when men
are afraid of the light."
—Plato

————— FEAR NOT —————

Not too long ago, as a board observer (no voting rights) representing a group of investors, I attended a board meeting for a software platform provider serving the manufacturing industry.

Over the past months, based on the input from the business units and data gathered, Brian, the Chief Strategy Officer had shaped alternative corporate strategies. He had met with various members of the management team and influencers. He had played the game of give and take by balancing organizational power, being sensitive to the corporate politics, and making sure everyone was happy—like the kind of pork barrel game played in Congress; I vote for this bill if you give me that. In the past few weeks, Brian had expanded his efforts by having one-on-one sessions with the board members, securing the votes.

Prior to that day's meeting, I had a number of conversations with board members and a couple of one-on-one sessions with Brian. The board members were all seasoned professionals with impressive résumés. Brian, an Ivy League JD/MBA and a veteran strategy consultant was also impressive. **But in retrospect, they were all addicted to the way things were done in the past.**

The official marching orders from the board and the CEO were to grow top-line revenues by 17% and enhance performance (cut costs) by 10%. To hit the targets, the planning journey had started close to a year before. Brian had assembled an "A" team to examine corporate strategy and answer the big questions: where should we go from here? How should we beat the competitors? And where should we invest our money?

Brian's team had worked with various corporate managers to develop strategies and business plans—solid budgets, defensible arguments, and ambitious execution targets. Each business unit contemplated new products and offered means of cutting costs through automation or layoffs. Mountains of data were gathered, customers were surveyed, and employees were asked to offer improvement ideas.

It took months for the business units to access and organize the data and months to make sense out of it. The consequence: they started thinking about the future based on old and stale data. Imagine a doctor prescribing medicine based on a patient's year-old lab results when the patient did not even have the symptoms.

In my briefings prior to the board meeting, Brian had emphasized that we can only plan around what is known and must commit to a singular strategy, then put investments and enthusiasm behind a forceful execution. Votes have been secured and consensus has been built, he victoriously claimed; the board meeting was an academic exercise needed only to officially record the votes.

Brian's addiction to a pre-formatted and static approach to planning was in line with the board members' expectations and their addictions to habitual approaches and process.

*In all, 10 months had passed before the strategy was shaped and an execution team mobilized. In the meantime, the world had been moving and changing. **By the end of the board meeting, we had an excellent strategy . . . for the year before!***

What happened here? Three things: a strategy based on old and static information was approved; consensus solutions as opposed to the most compelling strategy were adopted; and the internal power structure was reinforced. The company was committed to a single path forward—designed to ignore the constantly shifting marketplace. This is a process most companies go through, simply because it is the way they have always done it.

What followed? Millions were spent on execution. The company had to go through a significant financial restructuring and more money was invested. Brian moved to another tech company.

BIASES
BUDGETS
COMFORT
PROCESSES
FEARS
GUT FEEL
ORTHODOXIES
OLD ASSUMPTIONS
ADDICTIONS

The strategy was safe and comfortable but lacked the ability to adapt. The competition was months ahead before the company even started to execute. It was a strategy driven by budgets and artificial targets. The company's board and management had agreed to preserve their leading market position.

They chose to be methodical and secure in their plans and actions; but they should have been aware of the uncertainties and prepared to tolerate insecurity. They were addicted to a stale and static process, while the world they were competing in was rapidly changing and dynamic.

The new generation of CEOs suggests "stay hungry and stay foolish" (Steve Jobs, Apple); "Move fast and break things" (Mark Zuckerberg, Facebook); "most companies that are great at something don't become great at new things, because they are afraid" (Reed Hastings, Netflix). However, established approaches to strategy and execution are intended to achieve certainty and minimize risk. They are designed to steer away from breaking things, subdue creative foolishness, and submit to fear. They are methodical, sequential, and measured. They are anchored in the past— in planning, in aspiration, and in execution. Strategies are shaped by leaders who surround themselves with other leaders (board members) who share the same addictions.

There is a compounding effect of being wrong—**break the cycle**. Fear not what could happen if you leave your old ways (addictions) behind, fear what awaits if you don't!

Adam Grant, Wharton professor and *New York Times* bestselling author, in his book the "Originals" asked tech icons ranging from Larry Page and Elon Musk to Jack Dorsey and Mark Cuban about their entrepreneurial journey. Grant suggests that "They all felt the same fear of failure that the rest of us do. They just responded to it differently. . . . When most of us fear failure, we walk away from our boldest ideas. Instead of being original, we play it safe, selling conventional products and familiar services. But great entrepreneurs have a different response to the fear of failure. Yes, they're afraid of failing, but they're even more afraid of failing to try. . . . Throughout history, the great originals have been the ones who failed the most, because they were the ones who tried the most."

—— SEEDS OF DESTRUCTION ——

"It wasn't raining when Noah built the ark."
—Howard Ruff

The best time to induce change is when things are good. That is the time to experiment, to learn, and to discover your next advantage. That is the time when you have more control over your evolution. Many companies rise or fall with the economy. The delayed awakening happens during downturns—searching for costs to cut or markets to tap into in order to survive. There is comfort in making a little profit and coasting along. But the danger is to face the next down turn unprepared or worse, to never realize your full potential.

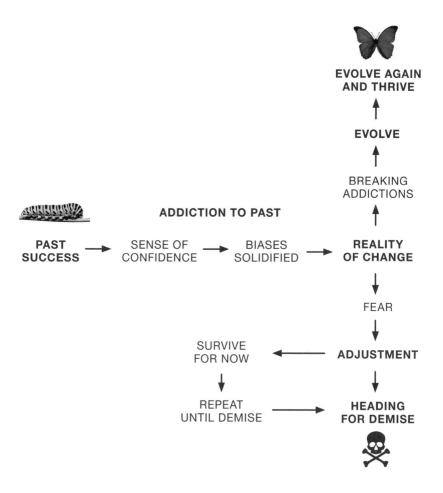

When faced with the reality of change, our past successes and biases trigger fear, provoking us to pursue a path of survival. We make process adjustments as opposed to breaking from our addictions and initiating a purposeful evolution. The caterpillar aims to be a butterfly, an entirely different species, and not just an insect that survives another day or two—that is its edge.

Being addicted to the past is not a function of the leader's smarts, hard work, or previous successes—again, this disease does not discriminate. As Bill Gates puts it, "Success is a lousy teacher. It seduces smart people into thinking they can't lose." Unfortunately, in most cases the seeds of destruction are sown in your success. Failures are often built on a foundation of old orthodoxies, beliefs, and practices—the principles and biases that fueled past victories may no longer be viable.

Our biases create a massive force against change. Meissner, Sibony, and Wulf from McKinsey claim that "two particular types of bias weigh heavily on the decisions of large corporations—confirmation bias and overconfidence bias." Confirmation bias leads us to more easily accept what is in line with our beliefs and ignore any conflicting information. Overconfidence tricks us into making decisions that are not rooted in the realities of our capabilities. Both are side effects of our addictions and both must be overcome.

Confirmation bias is how psychologists and economists explain "disappointment," where what is expected is not validated. American car company executives in the 70's and 80's assumed that their theories of markets and production were absolute. Newspaper executives presumed that an "editor is an editor," and journalism is the same whether online or in print. Neither group of executives looked to disprove their ideas nor descend from conventions. To break the cycle of addiction, begin with disproving yourself (if you think decision A is right, look for data points and reasons to disprove it in support of an alternative decision)—aim to challenge your assumptions and counter your decisions. If you can't refute them, you are acting out of intelligence and if they don't uphold, your decisions were habit driven.

Overconfidence, the child of arrogance, is the product of two factors: i) giving the information you have too much weight (e.g., I have years of experience, things just work like this in my industry and I know my people and my customers), or ii) resisting the knowledge that you don't know and having trouble imagining other ways of framing the future (e.g., using an internet site to buy a book, watch a movie, rent a room, or get a cab).

Other biases influencing our decisions, include "group thinking bias" as we get desperate to build consensus; "status quo bias" as we avoid the pressure of change; and the "now bias" as we push for immediate results (going for the low hanging fruits). All these biases are anchored in our outdated beliefs, in our unexamined perceptions, and in the insecurities that caused our addictions in the first place.

THE STATE OF CORPORATE AFFAIRS

Our institutional ways reinforce our biases and magnify the resistance to change. In most companies, employees and executives alike are invested in and protective of their planning practices. The budgeting process, the enemy of innovation, agility, and change, drives the timelines, decisions, and actions. Processes are guided by templates—ideas have to fit into predefined slots, or be set aside. You must conform to procedures, spend hours and hours on PowerPoint creation and filling out forms, or find yourself without the needed resources to operate effectively. Additionally, despite advertised initiatives and mantras, failure is still viewed as toxic and must be avoided. It is safer to submit to the organizational habitual beliefs and practices than to risk failure.

So year after year, we contain innovation to conform to norms, fill in the forms masterfully, overshoot on budgets and then compromise, and effectively focus on a future that is, not so surprisingly, very similar to our past. And that is the state of corporate affairs in most organizations today.

Recent A.T. Kearney research shows that 62% of executives see the strategy formulation process as much more challenging than a decade ago. Over 75% of those surveyed claimed that they spend more time on planning than before. Over 80% of the senior executives reported to be satisfied with the planning results; but, tellingly, close to half of management and employees doubt effectiveness—they simply don't believe executives have devised the right strategies. The study also showed that strategies are perceived to fail because they are top down and isolated (not reflecting the reality of market and company capabilities) and they are based on accepted wisdom and trending of the past (old habits and biases).

Mona Vernon, the head of Thomson Reuters Labs and a rising corporate leader who focuses on blending data analytics and corporate strategy suggests that, "there are some fundamental assumptions about annual planning cycles that are really flawed. The annual planning cycle is rooted in a world where a lot of assumption around competitive advantage, particularly for large companies, was rather consistent . . . . Today, cycle time and the competitive pressures are different. I am not sure in today's market how you can function with a static plan anymore, it is a bit risky." Break the cycle—manage your risk by planning more dynamically and evolving relentlessly.

Again from Vernon, "Monsanto spent about $900 million buying a climate centric technology company delivering data products for farmers. If you are the competition looking at this acquisition and what it really means: do you want to wait for the next annual planning cycle to come up with a response? Probably not!"

Larry Page, the CEO of Alphabet (formerly CEO of Google), suggests that companies often fail because "they usually miss the future." Thomas Edison, way back in the early 20th century, asserted that opportunity is missed by most people "because it is dressed in overalls and looks like work." Changing the state of the union, destroying your addictions, and embracing the future with a different way of thinking and doing is hard work. Don't miss the future, the work is worth it.

A surgeon can operate on a patient using the most advanced non-invasive methods and devices to increase the chances of success, reduce recovery time, and lessen the patient's discomfort. The doctor can be more precise in her diagnoses based on improved testing, enhanced instrumentation, and better data. She can be more targeted in treatment and much more effective in helping the patient achieve sustainable health.

Alternatively, the same instruments used decades ago can be employed in a multi-hour operation, risking the patient's life. The doctor can use her experience to guess the source of the ailment based on anecdotal symptoms. She can treat the patient the old-fashioned way because that is comfortable or because the nurses in the operating room are used to it.

The patient's symptoms and disease are the same,

but the way care is provided and health is regained is vastly different. You, the leader, are the doctor and the patient is your company. The old way of leading, strategizing, managing, and executing may be comfortable for you and your team, but it puts the patient at unwarranted risk.

Victor Hugo once said, "Nothing else in the world . . . not all the armies . . . is so powerful as an idea whose time has come." **It is time to change.**

You must alter your behavior and methods and not trust that past successes indicate the path to future wins. Balance the consistency needed to measure performance and manage the day-to-day with the imagination required to lead and surpass foes.

When addicted, we justify our behavior and actions using the "consistency" excuse. Bernard Berenson, the American historian, claimed, "Consistency requires you to be as ignorant today as you were a year ago." Oscar Wilde called consistency, "the last refuge of the unimaginative." Don't be historically ignorant and unimaginative. Don't use consistency as an excuse.

FIRST, ADMIT YOU HAVE A PROBLEM

The threat is real whether you are an aspiring entrepreneur with dreams of riches running a start-up or a well-compensated CEO at the helm of a formidable enterprise.

Many believe that addiction is a consequence of one's insecurities and is progressive, becoming more destructive over time. First, admit that you are addicted. Next, shift your thinking and actions. Be insecure about your future and get addicted to change and constant "Ahas."

Choose comfort and sameness and risk extinction. Or, embrace a world ruled by flux and filled with untapped advantages. Get the Caterpillar's Edge: evolve, evolve again, and become a butterfly. ... *Live with "Aha."*

"I must be cruel, only to be kind."

—William Shakespeare

CHAPTER 2
LIVING WITH "AHA!"

To win in business, first and foremost, you must change your perspective and actions.

Data, analytics, intelligence, and insights are not enough to win. Good strategy and flawless execution do not guarantee a win either. Our old comfortable approach to planning and conquest no longer produces the best results because the competitive landscape today is considerably faster and less forgiving.

———

"If the rate of change on the outside exceeds the rate of change on the inside, the end is near."

—Jack Welch

———

LADIES AND GENTLEMEN, START YOUR ENGINES!

Driving a high-performance race car is very different from driving your car. A street car and a race car both have four wheels, two axels, and brakes—but that may be where the similarities end. Street cars are built for endurance, safety, and reliability. Race cars are built for performance: engines are re-built frequently; suspension is often fine-tuned; and tires are changed according to conditions and wear—all in order to increase the odds of winning.

The race car driver and the pit crew coordinate as a team. Meanwhile, the vehicle's instruments provide critical real-time data (speed, oil pressure, RPMs, etc.). A NASCAR race demands split-second decisions—the smallest movement can determine the difference between a crash and a victory.

The underlying principles of driving a street car and a race car may be the same (hands on the wheel, foot on the accelerator or brake, sighting turns through the windshield), but the level of expertise, the concentration, the attention to detail, and the need for seamless teamwork makes driving in a NASCAR race a fundamentally different experience.

Bruce Leslie McLaren was a New Zealand race car designer, driver, engineer, and inventor. As a nine-year-old, he contracted Perthes disease in his hip that left his left leg shorter than the right. Nonetheless, Bruce entered his first competition at 14 years old. He was a competitive driver, but in many ways his legacy, the McLaren Racing Team, is testimony to his abilities as an analyst, an engineer, and a manager. His words confirm his commitment to excellence, "To do something well is so worthwhile that to die trying to do it better cannot be foolhardy. It would be a waste of life to do nothing with one's ability, for I feel that life is measured in achievement, not in years alone." Bruce McLaren's winning spirit is captured in the McLaren F1 race car.

The McLaren F1 is one of the fastest production cars ever made. The title of "world's fastest production car" is constantly in contention, but F1 is most certainly a feared and formidable contender.

Each McLaren F1 car has 160 sensors to capture performance data in real time. 2GB of data is captured by sensors and delivered to the pit crew each and every second of the race and to "Mission Control" at McLaren Technology Center in the United Kingdom—that is equivalent to over a half million pages of plain text every second!

Advanced technology brings together live and historic data. Over 250,000 simulations are run every second that help build strategies which respond to hundreds of variables such as weather, fuel, braking patterns, and tire pressure. McLaren claims "out of all this complexity comes one thing—absolute clarity on the next course of action needed to optimize performance."

Winning a race at high speed is about superior engineering, extraordinary collaboration among the team, great intelligence, and fast and flawless actions. In today's complex and fast-moving world, your organization is a high-octane race car, and you are the high-performance driver.

The point is: be a committed race driver, climb aboard, start your engine, stay alert, get informed, collaborate, and be agile.

—— THE "REAL" REALITY SHOW ——

The age-old recipe for success was to gather data, analyze it, hypothesize around insights, choose the best plan, and then execute that plan for the ensuing years. Today, this simply will not work. Why? Because set plans are by definition static, and the world in which we live and compete is dynamic, changing constantly. New technology allows for data points to come in from everywhere, all the time. If competitive business life were a movie, static plans would be based on only a few single frames of that film.

When I was 12 years old living in Iran, my father had an employee with a 10- year-old son who often visited my dad's office after school. I was jealous of him because he could tell me about every movie within days of release. How could he afford to see every movie when I, son of the boss, would have to save my allowance for weeks to afford one ticket? My curiosity turned me into Sherlock Holmes and one day I followed him. He walked to the movie theater and stopped at every window carefully studying each and every promotional poster. He would stare at one, then move to the next and then back to the first and so on. He took his time and appeared thoughtful and meticulous.

The next day, he told me every detail of the movie, including the ending. That same day, I saw the movie myself and to my amazement his tale was rather accurate. He may have missed some details but with his phenomenal imagination he had sewed together the few frames captured on the posters to get the story and the ending right. I envied him and naïvely predicted greatness in his future.

Over the years, however, I have learned that in real life and in business, regardless of imagination (what some veteran executives label "gut feel"), the ending of the competitive story cannot be gleaned from disjointed and anecdotal information. Besides, the ending of a story that has not been written cannot be assumed. You must understand each frame, its message and characters; you may predict a few frames ahead but attempting to guess the ending of a continuous, interactive, reality business show is an exercise in futility. In the movie of your business, there are customers, competitors, innovators, global economies, governments, financiers, investors, partners, and societies all in flux at all times —all with their own agendas, and all aiming to win the game.

Normally there are 24 frames (still pictures) in every second of a movie. On average, there are over 120,000 pictures (with sound) stitched together to tell a story in a full-length 90 minute movie. Can you tell the plot or the ending by examining only a couple of silent frames?

You compete for markets, customers, ideas and profit around the globe 24 hours a day. Your business movie has over 12,000,000 frames every year and each frame can offer insight into the plot. Can you be certain what the next frame in the movie of your business will look like?

The point is: it is foolish to believe that the full story (competition, markets, and opportunities) can be captured in a fixed plan based on stale information—but this is the very planning process to which we are addicted.

Plan and act as fast as the world moves. Assess and embrace the realities of markets, competitors, and capabilities faster and much more in-depth than before. Market advantage does not wait for the planning cycle. The world will not wait while you: contemplate, take time to gather enough data to be exhaustive in your analysis, and then build consensus around actions. Improve your likelihood of winning by **constantly** reading and applying the incoming data points. By always collecting and harnessing intelligence, you **always** increase the odds of winning.

At all times, be ready to shift your focus in order to position for a new advantage. Move faster to reach the moments of insight, where the solutions to problems become clear . . . those "Aha" moments. Don't be satisfied with only one "Aha" moment during a planning meeting or budget cycle. Terrific ideas are not about the annual off-site —they're about **every** day at the office!

THE GENERALS AND THE SOLDIERS

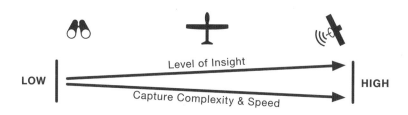

INTELLIGENCE GATHERING
METHODS HAVE CHANGED BUT OBJECTIVES HAVE NOT

In war as in business, access to fresh intelligence, smart planning, and swift movement is essential.

At the battle of Marathon, a runner delivered that

crucial message to save the city. Then, it was a horseman, a carrier pigeon, a single engine plane, or Morse code that delivered critical intelligence. Today, drones, satellites, and networked computers in "the cloud" do the job.

Of course, once the information arrives, it must be properly interpreted, never an easy task in itself. The master war strategist, Carl von Clausewitz, said that "intelligence reports in battle are often contradictory; many are false, and most are uncertain." He advised that, "even though our knowledge of circumstances improves, our uncertainty, instead of having diminished, only increases." Consequently, he believed that, "we do not gain all our experience at once, but by degrees." He emphasized the need for generals and soldiers to have "presence of mind," or an increased capacity to deal with the unexpected. Clausewitz recommended that apart from keeping armies at the ready, leaders' minds must also and always be "at arms." To be "at arms" is to: be ready to change direction, plan on a new course, pivot strategies, reallocate resources, and then execute without hesitation.

To win more often, take a lesson from Clausewitz, have presence of mind and always be "at arms"—alter your approach by seeking and finding those "Aha" moments constantly. Remember, every general was once a mindful soldier and every leader was once an attentive follower, be "at arms" wherever you sit in the organization.

To win, you must learn to live and compete in an uncertain and always changing reality. Winners are never too proud to change. That is why they win. Winners roll with the punches (giving and taking); they are dynamic, agile, and elastic, just like the world they live in. But this requires focus, discipline, and flexibility.

Winners prefer change to the comfort of stability. They prefer change to the ease of mind that comes with routines like: complying with planning and budget cycles; relying on stale gut feels; finding security in consensus; pursuing measured and incremental growth; and defending old plans. With comfortable routines comes the threat of extinction.

Charles Darwin claimed that: "Intelligence is based on how efficient a species became at doing the things they need to do to survive." "The goddess of the river," or China's baiji dolphin was declared extinct in 2006, joining millions of other extinct species who did not have the "intelligence," as Darwin defined it, to survive. (Even the goddesses can have a downfall!) The decline in the baiji dolphin population is attributed to a variety of factors including overfishing, boat traffic, habitat loss, pollution, and poaching—real and hard challenges to overcome. The cute and cuddly goddess of the river, the baiji dolphin, was also at fault; she was not "intelligent" enough to do the things she needed to do in order to survive. She could have genetically evolved to adapt to pollution, migrated to warmer or colder waters to avoid overfishing and boat traffic, or mated with other dolphins to protect her race —she could have been "intelligent" and changed, just like many other survivor species on the planet.

Corporate overconfidence, shifts in markets, change in customer expectations, better ideas, and hungry competitors drive many successful companies (the dinosaurs) to the verge of extinction while they may be comfortable with their routines and unaware or "unintelligent" about threats. Don't become the baiji dolphin of companies. Explore new competitive fronts and new products, services, markets, and customers; combine forces with others and look beyond what made you successful in the past—evolve to thrive.

The point is: prefer change and be intelligent—you are not allow to shift the blame. To survive, evolve and then evolve again and again. To thrive in business or in life, constantly look for the edge, the advantage, the "Aha."

—— THE "FOREVER EVOLVING" —— PATH FORWARD

Live *for* the "Aha" and live *with* the "Aha." In other words, let your mind be "at arms" always; don't imagine you know the ending of your competitive real-life movie, instead be aware of every frame; let your actions be intelligently aligned with today's opportunities and challenges. Look for the edge (a constant flow of "Ahas") that will help you survive and thrive.

To cultivate this winning edge, there are three crucial rules to apply. *These rules are simple to grasp, but difficult to follow.*

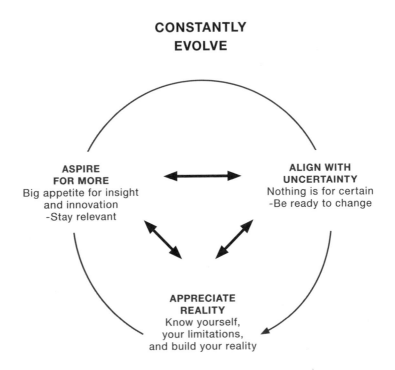

1. **Align with Uncertainty**—Adjust to the dynamic world around you.

2. **Appreciate Reality**—Understand what is practical and achievable by you and at your company.

3. **Aspire for More**—Seek more data, more analysis, and more "Aha" moments.

To abide by these rules you need a genuine willingness to **defy** the status quo. You need to **leave your addictions behind and break your static views and approaches**. But before your transformation begins, **let's get grounded**.

"To improve is to change; to be perfect is to change often."

—Winston Churchill

PART
TWO

NOT TOO FAST:
LET'S GET GROUNDED

"What counts is not necessarily the size
of the dog in the fight
It's the size of the fight in the dog."

—Dwight D. Eisenhower,
34th U.S. President

CHAPTER 3
THE TRUTH, THE HOOPLA, & THE BASICS

For centuries, thousands of merchants from India, Persia, and China traded goods with each other and with the Romans, Greeks, and Syrians along the 4,000 mile Silk Road. Each and every one of these entrepreneurs analyzed the market needs and cared about pricing and quality. Each used critical thinking, data, and analysis to strategize around buyers, suppliers, and competition. To win, they all obeyed the business basics and used data and analytics to make good decisions.

———

*"Know the rules well,
so you can break them effectively."*

—The Dalai Lama

———

THE TEACHER . . .
THE HISTORY

Strategy is the art of generals and leaders, the high level plan to achieve goals in the face of uncertainty. Until the 20th century, the word "strategy" as a way to pursue political ends through the threat or actual use of force, was reserved for military affairs. The craft of what we now call "business strategy" was first shaped in the early 1960s. Stanford Research Institute initially defined business strategy as "a systematic means by which a company can become what it wants to be." A few years later, R.H. Schaffer described it as "a means to help management gain increasing control over the destiny of a corporation." Business strategy was defined as the means of realizing a company's desires and gaining control over a company's future—a simple definition that still holds true.

After a period of academic pontification and debate, corporate leaders began to formalize processes and apply the concepts of military strategy to business. Their objective was to secure commercial wins in the battlefield of the marketplace. Subsequently, as success stories surfaced, strategic planning became the ultimate source of competitive advantage—a cure for cancer approach, a panacea for all ills of organizations. It was as if all those hundreds of thousands of merchants and business individuals over centuries had never planned to win and their success was purely random!

My father, as a recent college graduate and a bank
employee, and his brother, an army attorney, were familiar
with the challenges of poverty. Their desire for riches led them to
partner in an office supply store near an all-girls high school. Since
both brothers had full time jobs, they recruited their uncle to run
the shop—a one-eyed man in his late 60s who had grown up in
the bazaar and never got past the 6th grade.

In a few months, the business was booming and the
brothers were proud of their own brilliance. But the old
man was in full control: merchandizing, pricing, marketing,
and promotions.

One fall afternoon, the brothers visited the store at peak
time, right after school. The store was overflowing with young
girls and filled with a happy sense of hustle and bustle—the
sweet energy of business success. Observing from a corner, my
father noticed that a customer took a pencil or two without
paying. This was alarming! The one-eyed old man was clearly
not paying attention and could not see or control the theft. The
brothers caucused that night and decided to let the uncle, without
confrontation, go. After all it was not his fault he was senile!

Shortly after the uncle left, the customers stopped
coming to the store and sales dropped. At first, the brothers were
perplexed and scared—trying everything to no avail. Then, about
six months later, they closed the shop.

Years later, the disastrous ending was discussed with the
old man. A conversation that left the brothers surprised.

The uncle's success was by no means random. He was applying the business basics he had learned from childhood, working with merchants in the bazaar. He did not have an MBA or access to advanced technology, but was competing on analytics and timely insights. His success was well planned in every aspect, including the provision for theft! The business had failed not because the old man was senile or incompetent, but because my father and uncle were ignorant of business basics.

The old man had turned the place into an after school hangout (created an experience). He would selectively let boys in the shop—they had to buy or would not be coming back (a pay to play model). He was placing very inexpensive items at the end of the aisles to let the girls indulge themselves (a freemium feeling). As for merchandising, his relationship with a few influencer customers provided him with a constant flow of market intelligence about competitors (what they carried and pricing) as well as customer needs and trends (upcoming school projects and needed supplies).

Based on customer insight, he was managing inventory and fluctuating prices regularly (dynamically). Additionally, at the front counter, customers were teased with luxury high margin merchandise (driving impulse buys). In short, he was a world-class strategist, planner, and operator—applying methods considered "best practices" even today.

Creating an in-store experience for customers, demand-driven merchandising and pricing, and product-portfolio margin-management are not new ideas. ***Strategizing based on data and insight is not a recent discovery—it is basic business.***

In the early 1970's the legendary Chairman and CEO of IBM, Lou Gerstner, warned leaders about their approach to strategy formulation. He suggested that strategic planning often fails to pay off because: "1) everyone gets a warm glow of security and satisfaction when the uncertainty of the future has been contained—the planning period is over and nothing new now happens, 2) failing to give attention to present and future actions of competitors, and 3) understanding alternative strategies and the impact of change." Warnings that are still glaringly valid . . . 45 years later!

The 1990's thought leadership around strategy was dominated by Jack Welch (former Chairman and CEO of General Electric) and Michael Porter (to many, the father of competitive advantage, and a professor at Harvard Business School).

Jack was a proponent of getting to big "Ahas" and implementing like hell. His advice to leaders was to first come up with a big "Aha" for your business—a smart, realistic, relatively fast way to gain sustainable competitive advantage. Second, put the right people in the right jobs to drive it forward. Third, relentlessly seek out the best practices to achieve it, whether inside or out, adapt them, and continually improve. His recommendation points to the challenges of discovering an "Aha" worthy of pursuit and getting people and systems aligned to execute, while being ready to adapt to change. Again, challenges that are still germane decades later!

In a 2010 interview, Michael Porter said, "What I've come to see as probably my greatest gift is the ability to take an extraordinarily complex, integrated, multidimensional problem and get my arms around it conceptually in a way that helps, that informs, and empowers practitioners to actually do things." He provided the framework ("Five Forces") for people to follow—a road map for strategy, a kind of cookbook; a guide to outperforming rivals with a difference that can be preserved. Porter suggested that "strategy is the creation of a unique and valuable position, involving a different set of activities . . . it is creating a fit among a company's activities." Competitive advantage grows out of the entire system, and failure he claimed—it is triggered by managing independent functions and caused by constantly seeking operating effectiveness. He aimed to reinforce the idea that organizations are connected bodies and that driving for efficiency will not necessarily yield strategic advantage. Distinctions that, even today, many companies have a hard time making.

History, the great teacher, suggests that the basics of strategizing, blocking, and tackling have not changed over decades and perhaps over centuries. Strategy formulation has always been a lot more than tinkering with process. History also points to the source of failure: refusal to alter our mindset and approach in order to deal with change and uncertainty.

The challenge ahead is how to adhere to the basics of business while breaking the rules and detaching from old habits. Experts over the ages agree that good strategy is rooted in figuring out "what not to do." Apply that advice when planning for your future: choose not to strategize statically in a dynamic world. Decide to challenge yourself and alter your thinking and actions. Lip service around change and agility will not result in success.

"Going to church doesn't make you a Christian any more than standing in a garage makes you a car."

**—Billy Sunday, Baseball
Hero & Christian evangelist**

—— THE FUEL AND THE FORCE ——

Newton's second law of motion suggests that force is expanded as the mass of an object and its acceleration are increased. Force equals mass times acceleration ($\mathbf{F}=m\mathbf{a}$) and when either element increases, the force expands. In other words, faster speed of change imposed on a larger body of matter leads to an amplified force. That is the story of data today—more data created at a faster pace generating greater force.

More computing power coupled with the trends in digitization (turning data into machine readable format) has led to the creation of a tremendously large body of data (the mass). On the other hand, advancements in technology and shifts in consumer use patterns have caused an increase in the speed of change (the acceleration). The combination of these two factors has created an enormously powerful force that is opening new paths to insight and fueling innovation. This force helps "Ahas" be realized faster and advantages to crystallize more quickly.

More & More Speed = Larger Force of Intelligence

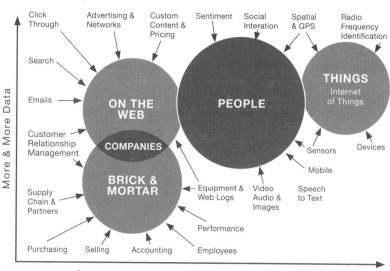

This force makes the process of strategizing much more complex and the advantages temporary. The force creates the impetus that can render established strategies not only inefficient but harmful. Some label this force "Big Data", the source of "Competing on Analytics." Big data provides both the energy that drives the need to plan dynamically and the fuel for the engines of dynamic strategizing.

Today, the force of big data and the insight it carries may be immense, but let's not forget that this force has always been around.

———

In the early '80s, analysts, using a good old HP calculator, manually tabulated pages and pages of financial and performance data to obtain insights. At the time, the data was too much or too "big" and mistakes always led to a huge amount of re-work. The invention of "Dbase2," a rudimentary database, solved this big data problem. The ease and expansion of use drove a demand for more power, speed, and capabilities. Again, data was becoming too big to process and comprehend with available technologies. As a consequence, companies like Oracle and Microsoft invented and commercialized relational databases—the big data problem was solved.

The Internet allowed people across the globe to buy and sell from their bedrooms—more transactions and more complex data generated around the clock. A

41

big data challenge that, once more, was solved with the next generation of technologies. Later, as people started to interact with each other in an unstructured manner (mostly by text)—a higher volume and greater variety of data was generated at increased velocity. Once again, new databases (e.g., NoSQL) and virtual processing capabilities came to the rescue, to solve yet another big data problem.

Ahead, is the IoT (Internet of Things) revolution—promising more and more data to be produced from all sorts of objects (e.g., electric utility meters, cars, watches, power plants, homes, cows, refrigerators, etc.) expressing themselves constantly. Yet another big data problem has been born and technologists are hard at work solving it.

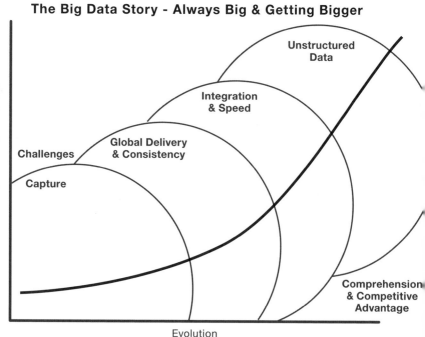

The Big Data Story - Always Big & Getting Bigger

Data has always grown too big and technology has always, eventually, solved the problem. Every time the data gets bigger, the force of its insight and impact also gets bigger. More data produced at a faster rate equals a greater force of insights, "Ahas," and advantages.

Steve DuMont, a former Cisco executive, a Middle East peace negotiator, and a CEO many times over believes that "the big inhibitor to being more dynamic in planning and execution is not big data or analytics . . . there has been a need for some period of time to be able to react more quickly and to change strategies as a result of massive changes globally . . . this [challenge or rapid change] is not something that has arrived recently. Almost for my entire career the concept of using data faster to gain over competitors has been around, and good CEO's have always used speed to their advantage." The major impediment is not big data nor Analytics, it is your mindset.

Arlene Harris, also known as the "First Lady of Wireless," is the first woman inducted into the Wireless Hall of Fame. She is a serial entrepreneur, an inventor, and a successful investor. "I am surprised why 'big data' hasn't been a big deal before now! . . . I was running big databases years back, looking for every way from Sunday to figure out how to optimize my operation or my revenues," Ms. Harris explains. The real test for leaders is not technology or size of data, but comprehension at a speed faster than the competition. The challenge is to see the

43

signals earlier and to understand the impacts quicker—to go from data to insight faster than the competition.

The force of insight from data is without a doubt massive and getting increasingly more powerful. Although technology facilitates the access to the force and the insight it carries, it does not guarantee a win in the marketplace. Advantages don't magically appear because we are "competing on analytics." They are a result of "competing on analytically informed strategies."

Fuel your strategies with a constant flow of innovation coupled with rapid and decisive actions. Put this force and its offspring, insight, behind your thinking and doing. Companies and leaders who push against this force are doomed to lose—to collapse and crumble. As Star Trek fans know, "Resistance is Futile."

The future will be ruled by visionary leaders who are not derailed by the hoopla of big data and analytics and are focused on comprehension, innovation, and strategy. Leaders who see information and data as a critical asset and not just a byproduct of doing business will gain the winning edge by discovering advantages and adjusting course as needed.

"The only thing worse than being blind
is having sight but no vision."

—Helen Keller

THE IMPACT AND THE CONSEQUENCES

To be clear, while competing on analytics, tapping into big data, and using technology are paramount to success in the future, a broken business model cannot be fixed by just massaging numbers. Don't confuse the truth with the hoopla. Big data, complex mathematical formulas, crunching numbers, or competing on analytics are not the cure for all ills of business, but the absolutely necessary diet and exercise.

A 2015 KPMG-sponsored research by *Institutional Investor* decisively concluded that analysts from every industry and sector are convinced that data and analytics strategies will have a profound impact on the companies they cover. Many companies deem their access to quality data, needed technology, and analytical talent inadequate. However, the survey suggests that investors believe that 78% of the issuers (companies) now have excellent or adequate access to high quality operating data and just shy of 90% have great or adequate confidence in the quality of the data. Additionally, over 75% of investors surveyed, rate issuers' analytics capabilities as adequate or excellent. In other words, whether you agree or not, those who value your companies believe that you now have a clear path to timely insight. Be aware, ignore the force and the insights and investors are prepared to penalize you with lower stock valuation!

When asked if they take data and analytics (D&A) use and strategies into account as they value stocks, 24% claimed that during the previous year they have done so and 45% (about half) indicated that they will somewhat or very heavily weigh in the D&A factor in their valuation decisions by 2017.

According to a 2015 Bain & Company study, the Communications and Media industry was expected to spend $1.2 billion on big data and analytics (growing at a rate of 40% per year). The Energy and Utility industry was anticipated to spend $800 million, growing at 54% per year. Leading the pack, the Financial Services institutions were expected to invest $6.4 billion in 2015 with a 22% growth. The study also suggests that companies that use analytics are five times (5x) more likely to make decisions faster than competition, three times (3x) more likely to execute as intended and two times (2x) more likely to have top-quartile financial performance. In a PwC sponsored survey, close to 85% of over 1300 CEOs surveyed in 2015 indicated that digital technologies are creating "quite high" or "very high" value through data analytics.

In short, a lot of investments are being made in data analytics and big data. All studies show that it is hugely important to competitiveness. Executives are by and large acknowledging its importance and institutional investors are accounting for it as they value public companies. That is the truth.

However, according to a March 2016 blog by Brian Hopkins of Forrester Research: "We wanted to examine the fact that business satisfaction with analytics went down 21% between 2014 and 2015, despite big investments in big data. We found that while 74% of firms say they want to be "data-driven," only 29% say they are good at connecting analytics to action. That is the problem." That indeed is the problem of confusing the truth with the hoopla—a problem rooted in leaders confusing "having technology" with "creating an advantage." An issue of mistaking "having data scientists on staff" with "innovating and strategizing through data and analytics."

———

Eric Schmidt, Chairman of Alphabet, warns that, "someone, somewhere in a garage is gunning for us." According to Upfront Ventures, the cost to launch a startup in year 2000 was about $5 million. Due to open source and horizontal scaling, the cost had dropped to $500k by 2005. Cloud based capabilities further reduced the cost to $50k by 2009 and abundant and cheap processing and storage further reduced it to $5000 a few years later. An investment level that allows many to innovate and become possible contenders.

The cost of computing is down by over 33% per year over the past 10 years and cost of storage of data is dropping by 38% per year (according to Forrester). The ability to process faster at an affordable price is here. The force of big data (or data in any form or any size) can be focused on creating fresh advantages all the time. However, research shows that only a fraction of companies (estimated 3% to 5% of companies) labeled as "transformed" are using analytics to guide their strategies. The rest mostly justify their actions with data.

Warren Buffet suggests that, "should you find yourself in a chronically leaking boat, energy devoted to changing vessels is likely to be more productive than energy devoted to patching leaks." Buffet also states that, "risk comes from not knowing what you are doing." Use the insight accessible through data analytics to avoid getting on a boat that is likely to leak in the first place (know and reduce risk). If for some reason external elements (competitors or market) cause the damage, use data and analytics to find out before it is deadly (know earlier and avoid risk). Have a series (a wave) of strategies and the willingness to quickly shift your energy properly (balance and overcome risk by creating options).

Ashwin Rangan, the Chief Innovation and Information Office of ICANN (Internet Corporation for Assigned Names and Numbers that controls the Internet's global Domain Name System) and the former CIO of Walmart.com, says that, "most people use analytics in the context of consumer level transactions. But there is no lasting strategic advantage. When people claim that they are competitive because they are using analytics, that's just the flavor of the day. Now unless you tell me that you have used data analytics in order to find a new product ground, a new design, and a new market, you are not strategic . . . as opposed to let's sell more shoes to the guys who are buying shoes . . . what is being done for the most part today is a kind of a tit for tat, and that's what I see most people calling gaining competitive advantage." Optimizing today's processes for greater efficiency does not necessarily offer an advantage for tomorrow. Use the force and create the future. Don't use data to justify your actions, use it to discover advantages.

———————

No doubt, the movement first labeled as "Competing on Analytics" by Tom Davenport (author and leading expert in use of analytics) is well on its way.

Across almost every industry, companies are using analytics in marketing, sales, logistics, customer support, human resources, and more. Organizations are forecasting demand, prioritizing leads, predicting customer lifetime values, estimating share of wallet, segmenting customers, and defining churn. They are optimizing sales channels and product mix, detecting fraud and minimizing credit risk, improving call center activities, and managing talent and recruitment efforts.

In Health Care, physician attrition, patient's remission risk, medication (dosage) effectiveness, plus nurse and equipment allocations are amongst many data analytics applications. In Retail, store location analysis, pricing, merchandizing, market basket evaluation, and warranty analytics are tackled, to name a few. In Insurance, agent and branch performance plus claims handling, and risk-reduced policy design; in Life Sciences, identification of Biomarkers and drug discovery; in Hospitality and Travel industries, occupancy optimization of rooms and seats plus dynamic pricing are widespread use cases.

In every industry, analytics is at the center of optimization. However, often companies are confusing gaining operational efficiencies with strategy. Although technological advances have fueled the nature and the scope of the analytics applied, the truth is that most of the activities listed above have been done in one form or another for decades. The force of data and insight is certainly bigger and growing, pointing to advantages that may be broader than ever before, but the real advantages are always guided by business basics and solid strategies. Don't confuse data and insight with strategy and execution. Don't confuse effort with results.

THE SIDE EFFECT: YOU ARE A FACTORY

Look beyond the data you have and explore the data that can be captured or generated. View "data" as an ingredient for other products or services. A farmer grows tomatoes, a retailer resells, and a restaurant mixes those tomatoes with meat and spices to make a marinara sauce. Think of yourself as a farmer and your data as your product. Or consider a transistor that can be used in a radio, a medical device, a spaceship, a drone, and a camera; think of your data as your company's invention, your version of a transistor. Think of how aggregating and combining your product (data points) can create new opportunities for profit.

The creative trends in monetizing data are real and the opportunities vast. Consider General Electric (GE) one of the 10 largest companies in the U.S. as they turn their data assets into a new business line. GE offers predictive maintenance and optimization services for more than $1 trillion worth of Internet-connected industrial equipment, ranging from medical equipment to jet engines. GE's newly discovered asset (data) was worth an estimated $1 billion in incremental revenue for GE in 2014 alone. Corporate takeovers are also starting to give serious value to data. Microsoft's $26 billion acquisition of LinkedIn "gives Microsoft an unprecedented level of data" commented Doug Laney from Gartner. He claimed that "it is all about data." Gartner's research indicates that, "companies that are in information product business have four to five times higher market–to-book value." Data is proving itself to be a valuable corporate asset and it is contributing in far more ways than just numbers on a corporate business intelligence dashboard.

Think of yourself, your employees, your friends, your kids, and your parents as "data factories." Everything we do generates data: driving a car, eating a meal, adjusting the thermostat, listening to music, watering the garden, buying a toothbrush, calling a friend, taking a vacation, getting sick and getting well. Everything we do generates data. Utility meters track when we wake up and turn on the lights. NEXT (a Google acquisition) knows if we are hot or cold as we play with the air-conditioning thermostat, Pandora knows our music preference for weekday mornings, Progressive (the insurance company) measures our driving patterns as we go to work, Waze knows the route we take, cameras capture our every movement, Fitbit (the wearable tech company) knows how many steps we take during the day, and banks and processing companies are aware of what we have for lunch. Our actions are digitized constantly. Each one of us is a data factory, constantly mass-producing data; a product valuable to companies, governments, social do-gooders, and thieves.

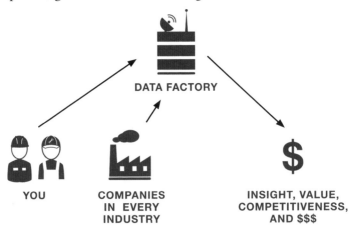

DATA FACTORY

YOU

COMPANIES
IN EVERY
INDUSTRY

INSIGHT, VALUE,
COMPETITIVENESS,
AND $$$

But, for you and me as individuals, what is the value to us? Can we benefit from what we produce in our data factory? We sell our time, why can't we sell our data? Will we have a "data" account like a bank account? Can companies trade our data or theirs on the commodities market? Can we exchange our data for goods and services? Can we barter with it? How about privacy? Will the power of ownership of privacy shift from companies to people? Has it already?

Each and every one of us and each and every organization is creating the fuel and the force of big data and of amplified insights! *You, your company, your colleagues, your employees, your customers, your business partner, your family, and your friends collectively are the force.*

——— MAKE HISTORY, ALWAYS ———

Theoretically, according to economists, in the last hundred years we have travelled through an age of "Manufacturing," where companies like Boeing and Ford shined. This was followed by an age of "Distribution," with star companies like Walmart. Next, we experienced the age of "Information," with giants like Amazon and Google as front-runners. Ahead, experts claim, is the age of obsession with "Customer," powered by big data—an era to compete on analytics.

In practice, companies have always survived and

evolved by looking for new advantages and finding new means and methods to realize them. Getting the right intelligence through tools is not new. Customers have always been pivotal, as has having the right distribution network and manufacturing capabilities; without ideas, products, and the means to make and deliver the goods or services you have nothing to offer the customers, and without customers who are willing to pay there is no business, period.

Obsessing over delivering value to customers is not a novel idea. Analytics did not emerge yesterday and data has always been big. Once upon a time, slide rulers dealt with big data, then came calculators, spreadsheets, and simple databases. As commerce on the Internet, social media, and the "Internet of Things" become more prevalent, sophisticated technologies such as "cloud" computing and "machine learning" take over.

Data is always growing and innovators have always found solutions to make sense of it. Through all the ages (manufacturing, distribution, information, and customer) entrepreneurs have used data across the organization to gain an advantage. As Elon Musk, the CEO of Tesla describes it, "If you're trying to create a company, it's like baking a cake. You have to have all the ingredients in the right proportions." To win over and over, you need to continually balance growth, risk, and efficiency by using people, processes, and products as well as data analytics and strategy in the right proportions.

Let's understand that a healthy organization is a connected organization where all elements are working together. Let's get over the size of the data and the complexity of analytics and focus on use and value. Enough with technical jargon and marketing hype. Realizing value and getting to an advantage is much more than clustering computers, building statistical models, targeting customers better, using tools or storing data in the "cloud." It is more than data scientists and business analysts massaging the data or constructing mathematical formulas. The reality of competition cannot be captured in mathematical formulas—not now, not ever.

Let's not just "compete on analytics." Let's "compete on analytically informed and dynamic strategies."

Not long ago, having a PC and access to an Excel spreadsheet was novel; it provided enhanced productivity—a distinct advantage. One day in the not too distant future, dealing with big data and analytics will be a matter of course. The future competitive landscape will level again as data analytics becomes a part of day-to-day life for all businesses.

The competition over analytics will soon be over. In sports, the playing field levels when the training, the equipment, and the home-field advantages are accounted for. In business, when all competitors can access the same capabilities and intelligence, the advantage is neutralized.

Soon, tools and techniques will no longer define the advantage and the business basics of good strategy and execution will, once again, drive the lasting victories.

"The best way to predict the future is to invent it."

—Alan Kay,
Computer Scientist

Make your own history and invent your future, constantly. Apply the basics dynamically. Don't deny the potential of the force of insight from data analytics, but don't rely on technology or data scientists to rescue your future. From the days of the Silk Road and forever after, in business it is always the age of "uncertainty" and the age of "flux and agility." Remember, the choice to shape your own tomorrow is yours—and it has always been that way.

The future belongs to leaders who have the will and the foresight to allow themselves and their organizations to use the force of data analytics as the wind in the sails of their imagination and innovation. The best tennis players understand that a good tennis racket may help improve their game, but will not make them a champion. The winners are those who acknowledge that knowing their own stats and those of their opponent in a baseball game or a presidential race can only help them strategize better. It is the strategies and desire to win that makes you a winner, not the technology that accurately tabulates the stats.

Business basics may need to be twisted a bit to fit the changing times. However, the proven power of business fundamentals should not be ignored. Ignore the hoopla and live with the truth that data and analytics help you make better decisions and dynamic plans. Make technology your ally—not just to improve processes or do things faster. *Partner with machines, for life*—broaden your knowledge, augment your intelligence, and expand your possibilities to innovate faster than your competition.

> *"The limit of your present understanding is not the limit of your possibilities."*
>
> **—Guy Finley, Writer & Philosopher**

CHAPTER 4
PARTNERS FOR LIFE

The age of the machine, abundance of data, and dominance of analytics is here; the time to apply these in order to focus on business basics has arrived; and, the era of data-centric products, services, and partnerships is around the corner. Resistance is pointless. Imagine a world without technology, then consider the impact on your personal health and comfort. Think of your company's productivity, innovation, and success. Is it feasible? Is it desirable?

"You may delay, but time will not."
—Benjamin Franklin

— AUGMENT YOUR INTELLIGENCE —

On a flight to Los Angeles I sat next to a young Marine—a future leader and a potential general in the making. Cramped in a tight space in coach, the vacationing

Marine and I got to know each other. Post-school and ROTC he joined a clandestine division of the special ops. Later, he became involved with "perpetual war games" while stationed aboard an AWACS—a $270 million Airborne Warning and Control System aircraft developed by Boeing to provide all-weather surveillance, command, control, and communications. Hovering over the world, AWACS's sophisticated radar equipment was constantly reporting the position and movement of ships, planes, mobile nuclear and missile launchers, and soldiers. What was not collected by on-board devices was flowing in from satellites and triangulated with the intelligence reported by the field operators. A fantastic assortment of data in the air—a dream come true for every data scientist.

The AWACS team was in charge of continuously modeling defensive and offensive alternatives—as the incoming information changed, their scenarios and outcomes would change. Based on trajectory of movements, probabilities, and signals, a version of tomorrow was conceived every few hours, allowing the experts to strategize dynamically based on real and present dangers . . . or opportunities.

"We must embrace technology to understand change," the Marine claimed, but more importantly, he continued: "all that technology and gadgets will not win wars, it is how we strategize using the insight and how we battle on the ground using all our people and assets. . . . Victory begins by gaining the *knowledge advantage over the enemy and keeping it." A lesson for all.*

In short, data, analytics and intelligence are critical, but it is timely strategies and focused actions that deliver the victory.

The science of strategy is to leverage machines and systems to extract insights from data quickly and understandably. However, the real competitive edge has always come from comprehension. Those who could get to insights and comprehend the "Aha" faster always have the edge—quicker to insight, quicker to advantage! In business as in war, to gain speed and expand your domain of knowledge, partner with machines.

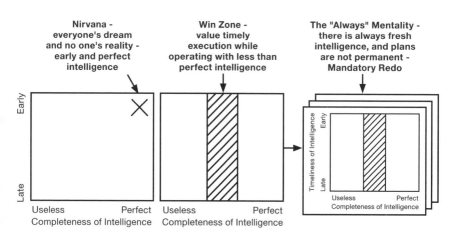

The artful part of strategy is knowing when to go to war and when not to; knowing where the enemy (the competition) is vulnerable and how we can, with speed, gain tactical and psychological ground; knowing when to defend a hill to death (stay in the same market and sell the same products) and when to let territory go (sprint to a different advantage). It is using data, extracting insights, deciding on probabilities, and acting constantly—all in concert as the battle progresses. It is identifying an actionable insight (Aha) and acting decisively—creating the advantage and evolving.

The secret to success is to effectively combine the art and the science of strategy. Victory is won through working together, as partners, with machines to bring data and analytics into focus. And by applying critical thinking in order to realize fresh advantages constantly through greater, augmented, capabilities.

———————

To partner is to share, collaborate, and drive towards a common goal—the fresh advantage. To partner with the machine is to recognize the capabilities (data and intelligence), computers and devices offer to shape decisions and impact actions. Augmenting your intelligence or "Intelligence Amplification," is about people partnering with machines to attain what neither can accomplish individually.

A classic example of augmented intelligence is a chess tournament organized between a chess master, a super computer, and a combined human-computer team. The tournament was won decisively by the man-machine team, comprised of a homemade computer and two not so masterful chess players—humans and computers working in concert to accomplish more. They won because they combined the computer's ability to process data to shape alternative scenarios with human judgment.

Like any good marriage, partnering with machines requires trust. Your aim should be to strengthen the relationship by understanding and accepting shortcomings. Don't expect the machines to fix dysfunctional business models or to magically create a competitive advantage. Use the machines to better yourself—but don't expect them to carry the entire burden. You must have an understanding of your partner—get to know the machines and what they are capable of. You can and should delegate technology execution, but never delegate learning about the full capabilities of your partner.

Gaining an understanding of machines does not mean writing code, re-wiring computers, or running clustering analysis in the cloud. Don't be afraid of technology—aim to understand the capabilities and limitations of your ally, the machine; the partner that holds the keys to the kingdom of tomorrow's insights.

As man and machine partner to learn more and do more, massive amounts of data (the next driving force behind corporate evolution) are generated. Every being (and object) can express itself through signals. By 2020, over 5 billion people and 30 to 50 billion (depending on your estimate) objects, armed with sensors collecting data and offering signals, are expected to be connected together. These connections constantly produce data and intelligence; they generate the signals that point to your next advantage.

Sheep in Wales transmit data to prevent agricultural pollution. The European Space Agency's Philae landing-vehicle announced its rendezvous with Comet 67P (4 billion miles from Earth) on Twitter, offering a vast amount of new intelligence fueling future innovation drawn from knowledge dating billions of years back. Cars sense danger and react before drivers; smart-phones identify a possible heart condition; apps conceive new award-winning food recipes; and more than a hundred million devices report readers' behavior on every book page, turning a solitary experience into business metrics and creative advice for editors. Insights, decisions, and advantages are rooted in the right data and the right (and timely) analysis.

Companies that own more of the "right" data (purposefully gathered, intelligently explored, and filled with timely insights) will have an edge. Those who partner with machines to augment their intelligence and capabilities can constantly learn and leverage their knowledge to advantage.

ACKNOWLEDGE YOUR ALLY

Lofty terminologies about today's business world abound: the digital revolution, the application economy, the fourth Industrial Revolution, the experience economy, the innovation stage, the age of obsession with customers, the period for the rise of the citizen scientists, etc. Jargon aside, these terms point to rapid change in customer expectations and technology, a reality that is reflected in surveys and acknowledged in management PowerPoint slides, but not truly acted upon.

Over 75% of 1,800 senior business leaders surveyed by PwC thought that they were making the most of their information assets. But, 43% (almost half) claimed that they obtained little tangible benefit and 23% believed that they realized no benefit whatsoever. Leaders admit the importance of information assets, but are unable, or most likely unwilling, to act on them!

"The real problem is not whether machines think, but whether men do."

—B. F. Skinner

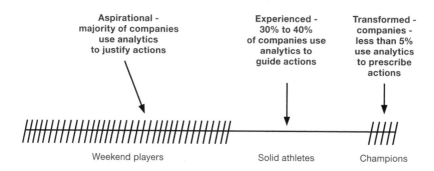

An MIT Sloan Management review and IBM Institute for Business Value survey of 3,000 leaders in 108 countries working in 30 industries found that the biggest challenge in adopting analytics were managerial and cultural. The study offered three stages of analytics adoption: i) Aspirational—use analytics to justify actions, a significant majority, ii) Experienced—use analytics to guide actions, a slowly expanding minority and, iii) Transformed—use analytics to prescribe actions, the very few (3% to 5% surveyed). Employing a data scientist, having a data lake, a massive data warehouse, and operating in the cloud does not make you data-driven, your attitude does.

Success is not a function of what kind of machines you have or how many mathematicians you employ. Success is rooted in augmenting your intelligence any way you can to discover new advantages and to act decisively every day.

In a Forrester survey, 92% of executives said customer service is a top strategic priority while 45% claimed they don't have the budget they need to get the job done. Digging deeper, Forrester mapped Michael Porter's Five Forces methodology against current market dynamics (the age of "obsession with customer") and found that every aspect of competitiveness is changing: i) the power of buyers is increasing as technology empowers them to buy smarter, ii) the threat of substitutes is more articulated as a consequence of digital disrupters, iii) people/employees are now the most valuable suppliers of ideas and they take them when they leave the company, iv) more is known about competitors with real time information and rivalry is more fierce, and finally, v) the barriers to entry are compromised as outsourced manufacturing and digital connections make new entry easier.

The point is: the landscape changes are not just about better customer service or customer targeting. The competitive impacts on all business fronts are life changing and leaders acknowledge it . . . BUT, interestingly, close to half the companies' surveyed claim they don't have the budget to deal with the challenges offered in this age of "obsession with customer."

Recently, the fourth Industrial Revolution (Industry 4.0) has been on the minds of executives in the manufacturing sector. Industry 4.0 is a collective term for technologies and concepts that pull together Cyber-Physical Systems, Internet of Things, and Internet of Services—a vision of the smart factory. By all claims, this is a defining period for manufacturers worldwide. However, according to a McKinsey

Institute report, the hype is not paying off, "six out of ten manufacturers are facing implementation barriers that are so strong that they achieved either limited progress or none at all." The top barriers, the McKinsey Institute report suggests, include: "i) difficulty in coordinating actions across different organizational units, ii) lack of courage, iii) lack of talent, and iv) inability to define a clear business case."

In other words, it is a big deal, but we fail to make progress because we are afraid of failure, have no imagination to crystallize the advantages, don't have the right people, and are not able to effectively lead and coordinate our organizations. Sounds like a bunch of excuses. Some leaders and companies are simply not choosing to evolve!

IDC, a research organization, believes that we are "entering the most critical period yet . . . the 'innovation stage.' An era defined by an explosion of innovation and value creation." IDC enumerates six concepts or technologies as the "Innovation Accelerators": Augmented or Virtual Reality, Internet of Things, Cognitive Systems, next generation Security, Robotics, and 3D printing. However, before you can accelerate innovation you must first acknowledge and appreciate the value of augmenting your intelligence and capabilities. Innovation does not simply appear because you execute a deal with the IBM Watson (Cognitive) team or contemplate putting a chip in your product to collect data (Internet of Things). Innovation is realized when what IDC calls "accelerators" are aligned with strategies, business models, channels, and corporate partners.

Spending on Cognitive Computing (the simulation of human thought processes in a computerized model) alone will top $30 billion before 2020 (IDC Research). SNS research estimates that the global spending on Internet of Things and machine-to-machine technologies will exceed $250 billion by 2020. On the other hand, McKinsey Global Institute research estimates that "Internet of Things" could generate $4 trillion to $11 trillion in value globally in 2025. Combining the three reports (only conceptually, not academically) suggests that for every dollar spent more than 10x to 20x the value can potentially be generated for consumers and the economy.

Don't ignore the reality of change and the role of machines. Choose to rearrange your priorities—align with tomorrow and augment your intelligence. ***Man-machine teams and adversaries are the future of business competition.*** Ahead, lie competitive battles that the digital natives, the millennial generation, or those who think and act like them, have a higher likelihood of winning.

CARRY YOUR WEIGHT, BE A MILLENNIAL

Who are these millennials? Customers, employees, and leaders. Being a millennial is a state of mind, anapproach to living and competing. Jeff Bezos of Amazon is a millennial. Larry Page of Alphabet is one. Elon Musk is a millennial. Jack Ma, founder of Alibaba, is a millennial. And of course, the first generation to come to age in the new millennium are millennials.

The millennial generation (the largest generational group in the history of United States) is comprised of those born between 1980 and 2000. There are over 84 million of them including 39% of the US workforce (50% by 2020). According to a PEW research study their top priorities are being a good parent (over 30% are already parents), having a successful marriage, and helping others in need. They are more educated than any generation before. They influence major family decisions. A technologically savvy group that exercises more and likes to work part time. They look for passion in their jobs and want to work for a company they believe in. They are capable of doing many things at once—they are considered athletes not position players.

In a 2016 article, Jeff Clifton, Chairman and CEO of Gallup, suggests that millennials are profoundly different: i) they don't just work for a paycheck—they want a purpose, ii) they are not pursuing job satisfaction—they are pursuing development, iii) they don't want a boss—they want a coach, iv) they don't want annual reviews—they want on-going conversations, v) they don't want to fix their weaknesses—they want to develop their strengths, and finally, vi) they don't see employment only as a job—they see it as their life.

"To some, millennials are perceived to be selfish, lazy, and narcissistic. They expect instant gratification and upset when they don't get what they want," according to Scratch, a division of Viacom, a list of not so flattering stereotypes. Anne Hubert's research at Viacom shows that millennials do not seek to rebel against authorities but rather like to work with them. About 72% of them are "afraid they are not living to their potential," while 84% are confident that "they will get where they are going."

Hubert's research also shows that this generation does not have a problem unbundling (picking and choosing) the services they receive from different vendors as long as they get the experience and results that delight them. They are not easy to please and demand more from life, society, companies, products, and services. They also expect more from themselves. They are "the first generation of digital natives . . . their affinity for technology helps shape their behavior", suggests a Goldman Sachs report.

Millennials are a "confident" generation—they expect more, believe they deserve more, and don't mind changing, switching, and evolving to get what they deserve. To win, be a millennial, seek innovation all the time, believe that you deserve more, be confident that you can get more, be comfortable with technology and change. These millennial characteristics are shared by today's super star CEOs. *Be a millennial, increase your chance of success.*

"Innovation distinguishes between leaders and followers."

—Steve Jobs

INNOVATE...
YOU DESERVE MORE

A successful partnership must enhance the capabilities of both parties. It must help advance a business or personal cause. A partnership must lead to value or it will eventually fail. You can help machines enhance their performance and create models and enjoy capabilities that do a better job in solving your problems. In return, technology can offer you a path to an improved situation—"Ahas" and advantages.

Comprehend and then break your orthodoxies. Then, innovate, experiment, and lead. To unleash true value from your man-machine partnership and get what you deserve, ***you must first position yourself to deserve what you get.***

To deserve more, start by deconstructing your orthodoxies.

Sunil Erevelles, Chair of the Department of Marketing at the University of North Carolina, says "Orthodoxies are a version of truth the organization has chosen to continue to believe in. . . deconstruct your orthodoxies before someone else does." Many companies fail because they over-invest in their old version of truth (their past) at the expense of future prosperity. The first step towards change is breaking from the past. Recognize your orthodoxies and innovate around them—re-visualize your future.

A KPMG global CEO survey indicates that the number one challenge for leaders, year after year, has been "staying relevant." The biggest risk in today's fast moving competitive world is "irrelevancy," not "inefficiency." To remain competitive, you must change constantly. You must reexamine your version of truth and orthodoxies continuously. You must fully understand what is "relevant" or better yet, be prepared to define relevant. You must innovate relentlessly, gain confidence quickly through experimentation, and lead the troops towards your next advantage without hesitation.

Hans Imhof is a Swiss-born engineer who worked his way up through corporate america and became a major contributor to the invention of Uninterrupted Power Systems. Unimpressed with big corporate business practices, he started his own company and built one of the largest of uninterruptible power supply manufacturers in the world before he sold it. Imhof has started over a dozen companies since then and has invested in many more. To Imhof "there are no more big projects, there are a lot of smaller projects . . . innovation all the time . . . the new norm is to constantly change and to get used to it; if not, you are in trouble . . . . Before one thing is finished you must start the new thing and then you start over again. You have no other choice but to experiment and innovate constantly."

Henry Ford is credited as saying, "If I had asked people what they wanted, they would have said faster horses." Innovation is not just giving people what they want, but giving them what they dare to imagine. Innovation is about recognizing that your customers demand more, your employees and investors expect more, and you deserve more, always.

Innovation is not an orderly affair. It is not a step-by-step, deliberate method of finding things out and getting things done. Innovation is different from incremental enhancement—it is about what has previously not been done or known. Innovation is the art and science of exploring (questioning) the unknown, unleashing the imagination, and discovering a new form of value—value that did not exist before.

Alice B. Toklas, a member of the Parisian avant-garde was being rolled into a life-threatening surgery when she asked her life companion Gertrude Stein, an American novelist, "What is the answer?" Stein replied, "What is the question?"

Answers are not the "answer." Questions are the cornerstone of innovation. They drive imagination and inspire innovation. While "questions" point to the unknown (what has previously been ignored), "answers"

only live in the domain of previously known (facts)—
where you can only aim for marginal improvement.

Stuart Firestein, the chair of the Department of
Biological Sciences at Columbia University, in his book
Ignorance: How it Drives Science asks: "are we too enthralled
with answers these days? Are we afraid of the questions?"
He suggests that "facts are selected, by a process that is
kind of controlled neglect . . . cultivate ignorance instead
of fearing it, understand the power of not knowing in a
world dominated by information." Ignorance (the world of
possibilities minus what is known) is about the future—a
guide to where we should dig for data, insight, Ahas,
innovation, and advantages.

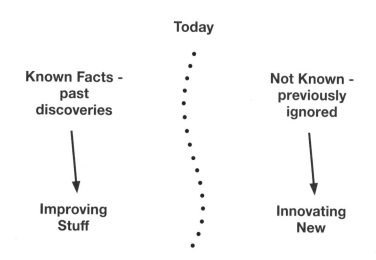

To innovate you must explore the unknown. Observation, hypothesis, and manipulation can narrow the field of exploration—help create focus; they may also narrow the world of possibilities—we focus on specific answers we seek as opposed to the range of opportunities. The innovation process should be centered on the questions we ask and not the answers we desire. The idea is not to ignore the facts or the known, but rather to re-imagine them as you leverage the unknown. Innovation is about entering the unexplored domain of ignorance and finding the pot of gold through intelligent, targeted, and controlled experimentation.

The process of innovation and experimentation is messy. To experiment is to explore the possibility of an advantage based on probabilities. To experiment is to make decisions based on imperfect intelligence—to operate in uncertainty and risk failure. To succeed in innovation you must aim to incrementally improve your odds of winning by experimenting and accepting failure. According to Winston Churchill, "success consists of going from failure to failure without loss of enthusiasm." If you accept the challenge of competing in today's business world and the need for constant emergence, then you must accept failure and regret. Innovation and experimentation require enthusiasm and commitment. They demand tolerance for failure.

"I've missed more than 9000 shots in my career.
I've lost almost 300 games.
Twenty-six times I've been trusted to take the
game-winning shot and missed.
I've failed over and over and over again in my life.
And that is why I succeed."

—Michael Jordan

Rita McGrath, a strategic management scholar, professor at Columbia Business School, and the author of *The End of Competitive Advantage*, recognizes that the world of competitiveness has evolved. In fact, it is constantly evolving. This evolution is changing the old definitions of manufacturing (think products produced by 3D printing), distribution (think e-books delivered by downloads), and information (think all the signals generated from billions of devices). Customers and their expectations are also constantly in flux. We live in a world where achieving a "sustainable" competitive advantage is no longer realistic and only a foolish dream. A world where sustainability is less about maintainability and more about the ability to re-invent thyself (to evolve, always).

McGrath's research shows that "rather than stability being the normal state of things and change being the abnormal . . . it is actually the reverse . . . stability is the state that is most dangerous in a highly dynamic competitive environment." She suggests that it is the end of the era of competitive advantage and old assumptions like "industry matters most." She offers an alternative view of strategizing and getting to results: to define where to compete, look at "Arenas, not Industries." Since every advantage is temporary and not sustainable, she recommends that companies have a wave of strategies (or a collection of strategies). She also recommends the pursuit of a more fluid and iterative approach to execution. Start with "Launch"—experiment on an "Aha," then "Ramp-up"—scale based on early success, "Exploit"— create optimized processes to benefit from efficiency, "Reconfigure—adjust to respond to changes in environment, and ultimately "Disengage"—move on to the next advantage.

McGrath's is an experimental approach that involves awareness of unknowns and constant innovation. This approach requires a different leadership mindset.

"I am not afraid of an army of lions led by a sheep; I am afraid of an army of sheep led by a lion."

—Alexander the Great

The leader, the one shaping the strategy, is the meaning maker, the voice of reason, and the architect of the future. She must be the ultimate fund manager deciding on allocation of company capital, the expert in identifying business disrupters (picking up on signals and change), and an operator who understands the challenges of execution.

77

Leaders should be committed to doing the "right thing" and not just managing by doing "things right."

Richard Rumelt (UCLA professor and author of *Good Strategy / Bad Strategy*) proposes that a bad strategy is not only the absence of a good strategy but also the result of misconceptions and dysfunctional leadership. Leaders who confuse goals with strategies and battle challenges with fluff and procrastination create bad strategy.

Leaders have always been a primary factor in success. But in the journey ahead, in this age of hyper-competition and flux, leaders are more important than ever. Good leaders are those who, in the words of Stanley McChrystal (retired United States Army general), "can let you fail and yet not let you be a failure." Good bosses help people imagine and passionately seek a better future. They don't claim exclusivity over insight and knowledge and are willing to learn, apply, and evolve at all times. Good leaders do not monopolize strategy and creativity. They are trail blazers who always want more, who feel that they as well as their customers and employees deserve more, and who know that they can achieve more. Role models are not scared to face unknowns. Good leaders are not afraid of innovation and experimentation. They are front-runners, who, like the butterfly, are not petrified of what they can become when they evolve and take flight.

Augment your intelligence by partnering with the machine. Acknowledge the value of the man-made and the accompanying data, analytics, and insights. Become a digital native and adopt a millennial attitude. Nurture your partnership with technology by breaking your orthodoxies, continuously innovating, and constantly experimenting and adjusting. Don't fear failure, it is part of life and competition.

Gain the caterpillar's edge by breaking the static. Embrace the idea that *your organization is alive* and unleash the power of uncertainty and change.

PART THREE

BREAKING STATIC:
UNLEASH & EMBRACE

*"When I let go of what I am,
I become what I might be."*

—Lao Tzu, Philosopher

CHAPTER 5
BEING ALIVE

Living beings and their environments emerge and evolve. The process they all go through is emergence (rise and renew) and all that they create is emergent and nascent.

The remarkable and unplanned patterns made by clouds and the unforeseen sculptures shaped by lava gushing out of a violent volcano are creations that arise from the interaction of life and things. The collective courage that erupted from protestors in Tiananmen Square, the commitment to country and excellence displayed by the Japanese after the atomic bomb dropped, and the remarkably fast progress made by a group of scientists as they created that bomb, are all emergent results transpired from complex systems. Life itself is an emergent result of interacting molecules.

Both you and I evolve and what we each create, our lives, is emergent. Our societies, the world, our organizations, and competitors are all unfinished and constantly changing—emerging. We all (people, companies, and societies alike) interact with each other and create our own unique patterns—our next future.

EMERGE: SHAPE YOUR PATTERNS AND PAVE YOUR PATH

In science, art, and philosophy, emergence is the process of patterns and regularities arising as smaller entities of complex systems interact—properties that do not exist in any of the pieces separately. Emergence is considered a source of novelty, creativity, and originality in art. Societies and economies emerge from the interactions between people, countries, beliefs, desires, technologies, resources, innovations, wars, competitions, and more. Your life is an emergent. You sense, learn, adapt, and evolve—you emerge. Sophisticated algorithms are embedded in your DNA and complicated physics, mathematics, and chemistry are at work in your every cell at every second. You interact with everything that is external to you to create patterns, decisions, and outcomes that shape your life. Living beings and all that they interact with create complicated and multipart systems—complex systems that emerge.

Organizations are complex systems. Companies are emergent. They represent a collection of human beings, processes, and practices—they are alive. A company is an entity that cannot be reduced to commonalities or differences among its people, systems, products, or markets—a whole that is not merely more, but very different from the sum of its parts. Each and every organization is distinct, represents a unique and integrated whole and enjoys a singular character (the company's persona). Each character emerges based on the behavior of its bosses and employees, capabilities, orthodoxies, collective imagination, systems, aspirations, partners, and competitors. You may study every part of it, but you can never confidently predict its patterns of emergence. It follows its own self-defined path forward. Organizations are always in flux, always emerging and always evolving. If they don't, they will die.

———————

In 2006, Ed Colligan, the CEO of Palm, discussing the possibility of an Apple iPhone, said "we've learned and struggled for a few years here figuring out how to make a decent phone . . . PC guys are not going to just figure this out . . . they are not going to just walk in." The same year, CEO of Motorola Ed Zander at a conference said "Screw the Nano. What the hell does a Nano do? Who listens to 1,000 songs?" as he dismissed Apple iPod. Both of these companies have crumbled as they failed to discover and embrace what is relevant. They saw the future as a continuation of the past and failed to emerge. In contrast, Apple has been able to emerge and evolve by innovating and changing. It has moved from being an anti-establishment, niche PC player to the creator and dominant player in mobile and portable devices.

Along the way, Apple has failed and been rescued multiple times. When ten years old, in 1985, facing a product and revenue crisis, Apple lost its inspirational leader and compass. After a period of turbulence and confusion with little real progress, a dozen years later Steve Jobs returned. The company emerged again in the early to mid-2000s as it introduced iPod and entered the music business by streamlining the online purchase process—offering a place to buy a song and a device to save it for replay anywhere, any time. Later, Apple redefined the mobile communications industry with the iPhone. It then evolved and thrived again as it introduced the iPad and reinvigorated Steve Jobs' lifelong core cause of making computers personal. Apple is an organization that has emerged over and over, with remarkable frequency, using innovation and boldness—a company with a unique persona that has constantly created its own patterns and path.

In 2016, again faced with challenges of declining sales and increased competition, Apple is getting ready for another metamorphosis. This time, without Jobs and with a slightly different approach—using investments and partnerships. Its one billion dollar investment in the Chinese transportation company, Didi Chuxing (the former Uber competitor now owning Uber China and an Uber investor), gives Apple expanded access to the Chinese market and a possible scaling path for an old Steve Jobs' dream of building self-driving cars. The investment also indirectly puts Apple in the playground with Lyft and GM (Didi Chuxing and GM are both investors in Lyft which is also an Uber competitor). Apple is positioning itself to emerge in a different direction!

Organizations are not alike or uniform. They are neither created equally nor do they emerge similarly. Apple is fundamentally unlike Microsoft. Both companies started in pretty much the same era and focused on the same mission of making computing personal. But who they are today and the journey they have travelled are vastly different. At the start, their commercial objectives may have been similar, but personalities, actions, innovations, and priorities made each distinct. Their reactions to external forces made them unique and positioned them to emerge differently.

———

Tom Fitzgerald, in a CEO refresher article, suggests that people have always instinctively known "that a human enterprise is a living, breathing entity, that grows and ages, sickens and heals, flourishes and fails . . . treating the company as a person evokes its personhood and simultaneously evokes attributes only living creatures have . . . like the ability to change and even transform." Organizations are alive, have a persona, and emerge. When a group of people (an organization) collaborates, interacts, communicates and pursues the same purpose, emergence occurs; a collective change happens, a fresh understanding that leads to new decisions, patterns, or changes in direction.

According to Patrick Conway, Chief Knowledge

Officer (CKO) at U.S. Army Training and Doctrine Command (TRADOC), in an environment where knowledge is constantly increasing at a faster and faster speed, high performing organizations must have a few characteristics: i) be adaptive (individually and collectively), ii) be innovative (solve the unforeseen problems), iii) be decisive (have confidence in leadership and vice versa) and lastly, iv) be committed to serving a greater purpose. These characteristics allow teams, armies, and companies to be emergent. Conway believes that "victory depends on morphing with time, needs, and challenges."

In the battlefield of competitors, markets, and customers, organizations compete to survive and evolve—to morph over time. Like a living being, an organization responds to dangers and acclimates to change. Just like humans, organizations are made of cells and organs (people and functional divisions) assembled together around a common goal. If they fail to constantly evolve and work together or confuse the common purpose, the results are deadly (cancerous).

Your organization is emerging whether you desire it, acknowledge it, or ignore it. The direction of emergence, the path of the evolution set by the organization, is a function of its collective purpose and desire. Its future is defined by how it deals with positive and negative signals—the decisions that lead to the realities it creates.

THE INGREDIENTS
OF EMERGENCE: LIFE AND DEATH

There are over 75 trillion cells in the human body and millions (between one to three million) die and are replaced every second. Some are lost through wear and tear, and others deliberately self-destruct. The body is always in a state of restructuring and flux, renewing and reorganizing. Through "Program Cell Death" or apoptosis, and based on programmed sequences in their genetic codes, cells kill themselves. When too little apoptosis occurs it can trigger cancer. Too much of it on the other hand could cause other chronic diseases like Alzheimer's or Parkinson's. A complex healthy living entity balances death and renewal—so should a living healthy organization.

Every minute of every day organizations, like humans, must renew themselves down to each and every cell; they must insert this need to self-define and redefine into their genetic code.

"In the animal kingdom the rule is eat or be eaten, in the human kingdom, define or be redefined."

—Thomas Szasz,
Professor of Psychiatry

In humans, red blood cells live for about four months but close to 100 million new ones are formed every day. Your stomach is replaced every nine days and your colon cells die after about four days. Living entities are genetically designed to self-cleanse—so should organizations. An organization is a collection of organs (people, systems, processes, and beliefs) working in concert and constantly looking for the path to emerge. Adhering to a new direction requires abandoning the old and the tired.

As an individual, you too are an organization with a mission, a set of values, and goals. You must compete and evolve on both a personal and professional level. The world around you is filled with change and uncertainty and is moving faster and faster. You, just like your company, must be always "at arms" and alert.

Constantly regenerate yourself and your company—renew, emerge, and evolve. Infuse the need for the death of old habits and orthodoxies into the fiber of your company. Make constant renewal a part of your organization's genetic code. Read the signals, appreciate the value of death, and purposefully kill your obsolete orthodoxies and biases. Eliminate whatever does not align with your next discovered advantage. Don't chain yourself, your organization, and your vision, to the past.

Competitive Life - Always Evolving

Regenerate Renew Redefine EMERGE

To renew your organization is not the same as eliminating your non-performing staff or offices. It is not about creating efficiency or reducing labor cost. It is about repositioning your organization with the right talent, capabilities, and insight to create the next advantage and naturally emerge to face tomorrow's challenges.

SIGNALS, CONTEXT, AND EXCHANGE

Through a complex network of nerves and synapses, every human constantly captures and processes data from his/her every cell and the surrounding environment. The data and analytics network and capabilities are collectively the nervous system for a living organization. As humans, we are able to process data, analyze it, and act upon it in real time; as an organization, we should aspire to do the same.

However, processing data and accumulating knowledge alone do not equal positive metamorphosis. Living entities constantly change their frames of reference in order to learn; they view the same situation (the same set of data) from different perspectives and discover more insights. The logo on a coffee cup suggests that it was made by Starbucks. When the cup is slightly turned you discover that it was made for "Sid." Turn it again, and know the contents, "an extra foamy latte"—same cup, different perspectives, added insight. Hear

89

the honking horn of a truck from the 20th floor of a New York skyscraper and it is an irrelevant and annoying noise. Hear the sound of the same horn as you cross the street and it is the very signal that saves your life; the same stimulus in two different situations requires different reactions.

Consider Google and Microsoft. When comparing the two companies from a perspective of leadership, culture, and innovation, you establish a base of understanding. If you look at the two companies by comparing growth metrics you will enhance that understanding. Compare the two companies based on their mobile platforms, spreadsheet tools, search tools, and gaming platforms and you will gain different intelligence. The collection of these insights captured by shifting your frame of reference gives you a knowledge advantage. No two entities, situations, growth scenarios, and competitors should be compared based on only one set of criteria. Limit your vision and your perspective and you will limit your insight.

To win, learn to change your frame of reference, constantly. Build a process to routinely discover and keep Connectivity, Consistency, and Continuity in mind.

CONNECTIVITY

Without reliable cross-organization connectivity through data it is not just probable, but inescapable, that "things will fall through the cracks." A "connected" enterprise is glued together via a nervous system that carries the data, and its crucial signals, to all organs or operating units. Get the departments and business units connected and then bond them to the dynamic world you compete in to get to a more comprehensive view.

Imagine the eyes operating independently from the rest of the body—feasible? Conceivable? The eyes only receive the pertinent signals that make them function effectively, while the brain receives a diverse range of signals from the entire body, including the eyes, and then formulates a response by coordinating these signals. The brain sorts, compartmentalizes, and deciphers the relevant data in a connected way—it provides context constantly.

For companies, the signals that have to be connected come from four conceptual buckets: i) "Performance"—signals pointing to your sales, returns, product quality, satisfaction measurers, equipment and people utilization, stock prices, profitability, and more, ii) "Capabilities"—signals that inform you of your ability to deliver: resources, facilities, intellectual property, distribution networks, partners, etc., iii) "Ecosystem"—beyond economic, legal and other uncontrollable factors, and impactful signals from adjacent industries (e.g., if people are getting used to free delivery in one industry, they are bringing that expectation to you), lastly, iv) "Market Dynamics"—signals that point to familiar factors such as supplier and buyer powers as well as competitor moves and behaviors. Collectively and in a connected manner, the signals from these buckets can help you gain more comprehensive and timely insights. Be brain-like, change your frame of reference, triangulate the signals, establish context, comprehend the insights, and formulate actions.

Connectivity is critical to discovery—when the signals are broken, effectiveness is compromised. In order to discover more "Ahas," view the organization and your strategies in a connected manner.

CONSISTENCY

To discover the "Aha" often, be alert and aware of the pulse of the organization; constantly compare and contrast realities and uncertainties through data. Discovery begins with recognition of change and identification of differences. (For example, have the competitors moved? In what direction? Are your capabilities on par with your strategy? Where are the shortfalls? Have the customers' needs shifted? At what scale?)

Consistency provides the very crucial base that can be trusted to judge against—you were there, now you are here, and this is where you are headed. If you lose consistency in data capture and analysis, you lose trust in what you may discover; and the ability to answer the critical questions of "how well are you doing?" and "compared to what?"

Be consistent in measurement and evaluation. But don't be consistent in the way you examine the data and look for insights—always change your frame of reference. Also, remember to be inconsistent in imagination and unbounded in your aspiration for innovation.

CONTINUITY

The value of what you discover is always a function of time. Find out that some of your cells became cancerous a year too late and you have jeopardized your existence. Figure out what tomorrow's news is today and you have unlimited financial opportunities. Time is critical. Time defines the value of insight and actions. It provides the ability to discover change and to judge progress. Time is the constant unit of measurement that applies to you and every division and function within your organization. It is the only measure that also applies equally to your environment, customers, and competitors.

Understand the change "in time" and you have a competitive advantage. Give context to connected signals measured with consistency—be fully aware of the impact of change over time (the factor that defines the value of all insights). *Your objective should not be to race against time (agility), but to plan a pace with time (strategize dynamically).* Understand the signals at the right time and in the right context and you have the knowledge edge. Act on that gained edge and you have the advantage.

—— LIFE IS ABOUT EXCHANGE ——

Every organization has a reciprocal relationship with its stakeholders (customers, employees, partners, investors, and the society)—an exchange of value. A company offers a product or service, an experience, or compensation, in exchange for revenues, stock appreciation, loyal employment, or committed partners. This exchange relationship applies to every organization, large or small.

As an individual, you constantly balance your priorities and relationships. You exchange value with your "stakeholders": parents, spouses, kids, friends, colleagues, and neighbors. You give something (your time, money, affection, knowledge, etc.) and get something in return (love, happiness, joy, health, respect, security, a paycheck, etc.). You balance this exchange depending on circumstances and needs: more time for a sick child or to attend a championship soccer game, more time for work as you face a deadline, more money allocated to kids in college, and more attention to friends on weekends. You exchange based on priorities, needs, and the nature of the relationships. If you fail to balance this exchange you have an unhappy spouse, a complaining parent or boss, or disappointed kids. Every action you take has an exchange consequence.

All corporate strategies and management actions have exchange consequences as well. If the value delivered to a specific stakeholder is less than she expects, she will react (e.g. customers leave when they don't receive the value they are looking for, stocks don't appreciate if investors lose trust in the future and go short, and employees stop giving the company 100%). *A winning strategy aims to balance the value delivered to all stakeholders at all times.*

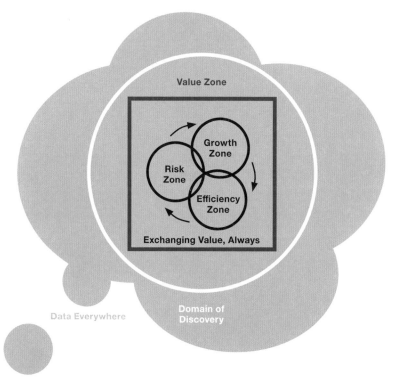

As you exchange value with your business stakeholders (customers, employees, partners, investors, or society) and constantly receive signals (about your performance, capabilities, market dynamics, or ecosystem) you must also balance growth, risk, and efficiency. The world is filled with signals and noise, to avoid getting overwhelmed narrow the universe of possibilities by focusing on the most relevant— the signals that impact the exchange of value. Group them, monitor them, and evaluate them in zones of value that are directly linked to strategy and performance: i) <u>Growth Zone</u>—where all signals impacting the growth of a company are maintained, monitored, and analyzed, ii) <u>Risk Zone</u>— where signals that affect corporate risk are observed and explored, and iii) <u>Efficiency Zone</u>—where signals related to corporate performance enhancement and cost containment are housed and evaluated. Organizing your data analytics efforts around these zones provides the ability to regularly measure the exchange of value and effectiveness of your strategy (not just financial outcomes).

Use a connected, consistent, and continuous framework for data gathering and analysis. Give it context by shifting your frame of reference to discover the insights and next advantages. Then, aim to understand the relationships between the signals, the insights, the contemplated advantages, the needed actions, and the value delivered to your stakeholders.

Remember, any strategy or action has a value exchange consequence. Aim to first understand the nature of the exchange and then measure its impact on your growth opportunities, risk exposure, or efficiency needs. The objectives: i) avoid getting lost in too much data and missing the "Aha" moments, ii) make your strategy align with the value exchanged between the stakeholders, and iii) focus and balance imperatives that impact your growth, risk exposure, and effectiveness, constantly.

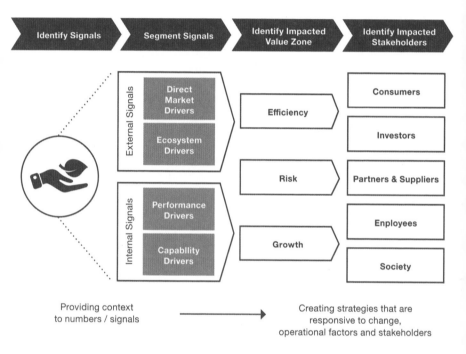

There is no unique version of reality and no single version of the future. Your path is defined only by your emergence. Your unique evolution is defined by how you view signals and insights and by how you imagine and construct your future. The point is that what you measure, how you measure it, and what insights you prioritize define how you emerge as an organization. Don't only measure by the number of times the cash register rings today, but also by the "Aha" moments that drive your next evolution.

"Life is not measured by the number of breaths we take, but by the moments that take our breath away."

—Maya Angelou

Acknowledge that your organization is alive, unleash yourself and your organization, and stand ready to emerge, always. Let your organization constantly turn signals into insight and action. Give it room to experiment and the confidence to emerge and redefine itself. Be conscious of the value your company is exchanging with its stakeholders and seek to balance your growth, risk, and efficiency as you emerge.

Ignite your evolution. ***Gain the caterpillar's edge*** to energize your future and start your renewal.

CHAPTER 6
GAINING THE EDGE

Acquiring the edge begins with a desire to evolve, a willingness to conquer fears of unknowns, and an honest view of reality; and it ends with a renewed yearning to evolve again. You, I, and our companies are *caterpillars* with the potential to be *butterflies*. Gain the edge; evolve over and over and thrive in business; make that your *mission*.

> *"We kill all the caterpillars and complain there are no butterflies."*
>
> **—James Marsden, Author**

MISSION ALPHA: UNCERTAINTY IS YOUR ALLY

Accept that to be certain is to be wrong. Admit that certainty is only reasonable probability.

In your daily life you are perfectly comfortable living with chance. You take an umbrella based on weather reports. You manage your drive to work based on assumptions about

99

traffic. You may even bet on football games based on odds.

However, in your professional life, you are expected to be 100% confident about plans and outcomes. You expect decisive strategies, firm directions, and measurable goals. You must be certain (or at least appear certain) because this is your company's livelihood.

A previously successful strategy does not guarantee a future win. The strategy may be tested and appear certain, but eventually it will make you a victim of your competitors. The desire to be certain (and confident in that certainty) slows down the planning and decision-making process. It also limits the ability to discover the most compelling opportunities. It actually puts your livelihood in danger.

Netflix, a young startup approached Blockbuster's management to sell the company in the spring of 2000 (for a rumored $50 million) in order to join forces and create the "click and mortar" video rental business.

Blockbuster's management, according to some observers, laughed them out of the room. Blockbuster stayed committed to their strategy and addicted to their old ways of doing business. They continued to rent movies on DVDs from stores. Meanwhile, Netflix changed the game. Although Netflix started by sending DVDs through the mail (thus establishing a subscription model for physical distribution) they quickly moved to emphasize an online model. Netflix went on to augment their vision far beyond the rental video market. First, they partnered with TV networks to offer re-runs of shows (e.g., ABC's *Scandal*), then they created their own award winning shows (e.g., *House of Cards* and *Orange Is the New Black*). Today, Netflix is challenging cable companies on entertainment value, price, and content; it is worth over $25 billion. Blockbuster went bankrupt.

Blockbuster is hardly the only example of a company focusing behind instead of ahead. Sony lost its leadership role in the music distribution and portable device business (the Walkman) to Apple (the iPod). Microsoft compromised their significant lead in the electronic games market (gained through X-Box and Halo) to online game companies (e.g., Blizzard Entertainment and World of Warcraft) by insisting that only their own proprietary device be used (a position they have now reversed—as of March 2015 game developers and players can plan for cross platform and collaborative games). Blackberry was the king in the cell phone business before it refused to evolve and respond to customer needs, handing the keys to the kingdom to the iPhone and the Android.

These companies failed to appreciate the force and speed of market and technology change. They did not watch, analyze, and react.

Today, old and established companies like Sears, JC Penny, and Best Buy are seriously challenged by the likes of Amazon and Alibaba (the Chinese e-commerce giant coming to America shortly). Traditional retailers are struggling. They are downsizing staff, closing stores, and playing catch-up by investing millions to figure out the online retail space. Financial Services (representing over 7% of the U.S. GDP) is facing major challenges as well. Banks are battling the forces of electronic wallets and mobile banking. Insurance companies are on the verge of massive change (i.e., a consumer survey showed that 67% of people are perfectly happy buying insurance from the likes of Google).

Companies live in a more complex and connected environment; their threats come from unconventional, unknown, and uncertain directions. Honeywell, a Fortune 100 manufacturing company and the self-proclaimed leader in energy efficiency is under attack by tens of fast-moving and innovative early stage companies (e.g., Nest, UniKey, and Simply Safe). The value propositions for giants like Marriott and Hilton in the hospitality business are being threatened by startups like AirBnb while the taxi local transportation businesses are being transformed by Uber, Lyft, and others. Even if you exclude early stage ventures, the lifespan of companies is much less than the average human's. There are not that many companies over 75 and unlike humans, the trend is toward shorter life. Twitter was once fresh, innovative, and a high performer, but based on a number of performance measures around engagement, content sharing, and active subscribers, Instagram is gaining fast and surpassing it. Visa and MasterCard ruled the world for decades (next to cash of course) until PayPal came along; today, smart wallet offerings are challenging all.

In short, old strategies are becoming obsolete and no company or industry is immune from this change. Embrace change to survive. Invoke it to thrive. Your mind is the architect of your change. When your judgment is clouded by past victories or by fear of uncertainty, you risk your future.

Ashwin Rangan, CIO of ICANN says, "The biggest challenge, especially if you are already successful, is the ability to get past denial." He continues, "It's very hard to do that when you are successful, because success is a potent sort of go-to-your-head medicine; it makes you feel lightheaded; it makes you think that you are the king of the hill; it can rob you of your humility. And it closes your mind."

The point is: today's business landscape is not forgiving. Winning in a more complex and changing world requires a more robust approach. It requires a mind shift. It requires an alignment with uncertainty.

*"We are a product of our past,
but we don't have to be prisoners of it."*

**—Rick Warren,
Pastor and author**

FORTUNE TELLERS VS. FORTUNE MAKERS

Because there are no crystal balls, you must learn to align with uncertainty as it unfolds, in real time. To "align with uncertainty" means to get comfortable with probability (not certainty) while knowing full well that change always lies ahead. To align with uncertainty is to keep up with speed, to stay alert, and to take advantage of the unexpected.

Chris Hoehn-Saric dropped out of Johns Hopkins University undergraduate program in early 1980s. Fifteen years later, he was invited by Michael Bloomberg to join the Hopkins' Board of Trustees. "He's a successful person in building organizations, and clearly he can give us management advice," said Bloomberg, founder and CEO of Bloomberg L.P., and three term mayor of New York City.

Hoehn-Saric's first foray into the world of business came early. While still in a Baltimore high school, he launched a small software company that wrote and sold computer games. Shortly after, and while at Johns Hopkins, he partnered with a friend to create LifeCard International—at 21 years old, he sold the company to Blue Cross Blue Shield for millions. The two young partners spun the money into an investment firm, Sterling Capital Ltd., today a $5 billion private equity firm.

One Hoehn-Saric company, Shoreline Education,

focuses on partnering with universities to create expanded student programs. Hoehn-Saric and his Shorelight team recognize the value of solid execution and acknowledge the need to change, always. Not because they are in trouble, but to increase their odds of winning. They plan to constantly evolve and have developed a process to deal with uncertainty.

"We are running multiple lines at Shorelight. One is an execution line—the team has to function in a certain way to deliver great service. The second is a multi-branched strategy line that lays on top—anticipating where we think we are headed, how the competitors may behave, and where the markets of tomorrow will be." Hoehn-Saric credits their success to, "Constantly staying alert to all data and information that affects the company (not just internal and performance data but external market conditions and behaviors). We adjust course, always positioning for the next advantage. Shorelight maintains a two-year plan and a five-year plan—both are continually examined and revised." He continues, "Our rapid and expanding success (winning close to four out of five opportunities in the U.S.) is a function of our dynamic approach to planning and execution—our ability to face uncertainty."

People who are anchored in the past work hard, they bet on their vast experience and instincts, and they are loyal to the institution and its routines. Matthias Muller is the CEO of Volkswagen (formerly division head for

Porsche, he replaced his mentor, Martin Winterkorn, after the emission testing scandal). He is credited as saying "we don't want a smartphone on wheels"—poking fun at the industries move towards smart and self-driving cars. Mr. Muller has a vast amount of experience, he is a tried-and-true car guy comfortable with the accepted industry and corporate routines. He challenges the vision (self-driving and autonomous vehicles) backed by hundreds of millions of dollars in investment by the likes of Google, Apple, Uber, and numerous Silicon Valley venture capitalists.

Leaders of the future work smart (with flexibility and creativity), relentlessly augmenting their instincts with fresh intelligence. Their first loyalty is to transformation and change. They have the fortitude to acknowledge that the world around them evolves endlessly. They embrace uncertainty head-on; in fact, they use it to advantage. All mechanical devices fail at some point, software has bugs and cars break. General Motors and Toyota had to deal with failures by paying billions for their recalls—they learned too late! Tesla constantly receives data from vehicles on the road and through analytics identifies and implements enhancements before issues impact customer experience. Your car is improved through software uploads while you are asleep overnight. The idea is that you will have an even better car when you are ready to sell it! Elon Musk, Tesla's CEO, is approaching a very static and slow moving industry with a dynamic and ever evolving mindset.

Acknowledge that the road ahead is uncertain. Plan around probabilities and in short cycles. Win more often by reserving the right to change direction, to pivot when needed.

Fortune makers embrace uncertainty and take advantage of it. They understand that the road to success is filled with twists, turns, uncertain challenges, and is "always under construction." Fortune tellers are corporate fantasists. They follow the trends of the past and project nirvana for years to come. They ignore uncertainty and hope that competitors will abide by their version of the truth (orthodoxies) and their rules of engagement. But be forewarned, *"HOPE" is not a winning strategy*.

—— THE NEVER-ENDING MARCH ——

Your own alignment with uncertainty is not enough. You only win as a team and emerge as an organization. You will need to guide your employees to change their rhythm with you, to think and act in pace with the world where you compete.

Recently a friend, an executive in the booming consumer security business, visited me from Europe. He expressed his excitement about a recent acquisition of his Paris-based company. He described the acquired company as an American success in cyber security—a young, agile, and focused company.

In contrasting culture and approach between the old

and established parent and the new and vibrant offspring, he offered a pointed story. "We had a major session to coordinate the integration of the two companies in the morning. The night before, I had dinner with their very energetic executive team. Then, on the drive home, thinking to myself, I realized that my colleagues and I needed to step up our game. I stayed up late and got to the office early the next morning. With a solid plan and agenda in hand, I called a colleague into my office. We discussed the importance of the session that was scheduled in a few hours and the need for us to put our absolute best foot forward in order to impress the new guys. I told him that my dinner with the group the night before had surfaced ideas and challenges we had not considered; in short, we needed to update our presentation and plans <u>before</u> the meeting. I asked him to help make this happen."

*In response, my colleague paused, had a sip of his coffee and said, **'I'm not a fireman'**—challenging the need for timely change and questioning the importance of staying relevant in one swift stroke. There is no need for us to change our ways or plan and act differently, he claimed. There is no burning fire. We have our people and processes and they can slowly adapt to it, he proclaimed.*

At that moment I feared our future."

If your house is not on fire (or you think it is not), it soon will be. Every member of your team must be a fireman, be ready mentally and physically to deal with challenges; or your house will burn to the ground, guaranteed.

If your people are not on board with agility and change, you too should fear the future. Panic if your organization seeks sameness and predictability. Your employees and partners must recognize that the company's strategies are fluid. They have to accept that no plan is ever absolute, secure, and eternal.

Lynne Doughtie, the CEO and Chairman of KPMG is doubtful that shorter planning cycles and a more flexible strategy process work without "changing the way we deal with the people side of things."

Recently, Doughtie, an expert in running large complex organizations, joined Arianna Huffington of the Huffington Post, Indra Nooyi the CEO of PepsiCo, and Virginia 'Ginni' Rometty the Chief Executive of IBM as one of the 50 most powerful women in New York. Before becoming the CEO and Chairman of KPMG, Doughtie led the fast growing $2.6 billion in revenue advisory practice for the firm.

Doughtie believes that getting people (leaders, managers, and workers) to accept that all plans are subject to change is both important and complex, "the real challenge to address is managing the workforce in a fast moving and uncertain environment." Leaders are absolutely critical to success, but true victory (tangible results) is only achieved in the foxholes by employees who change their execution tempo to deal with uncertainty.

Changing the rhythm and the tempo of the organization is neither easy nor trivial. People do not alter their routines randomly; people don't change unless they fear their future survival—they need to see their personal lives at stake. There will be no real change until employees actually believe that change is needed; they must trust that the proposed direction of change (transformation) is to their advantage.

The reality is "often executives become so tied to a path that all other roads are ignored" explains Doughtie. "Certain leaders and managers become married to a particular strategy . . . they see change as risky and that drives them to be defensive." Being married to the past and fear of change are diseases many leaders suffer from; contagious infections that can easily contaminate the rest of the organization. Don't rock the boat, they claim, not acknowledging that a steady and safe journey to a wrong destination is the real danger!

Does a caterpillar know how it would feel to fly as a butterfly before it becomes one? Evolution may be scary but it is essential to survival.

The massive onslaught of data and intelligence, the constant flux in a company, and the fierce competition in markets are all here to stay. Subsequently, strategies must be versatile and actions quick. It is of paramount importance for everyone (leaders and employees alike) to be prepared to adjust rhythms at all times, and repeatedly. *No exceptions. No excuses.*

But, simply demanding an adjustment in people's rhythms and outlooks will not produce results. Inspirational speeches, incentive programs, and slow-paced consensus building will not work either. You cannot force people to belong to or emerge as an organization, but you can stimulate change. You are not asking your entire company to adapt to a new set of actions and changes in order to fit into a new plan. Rather, you are asking them to change the way they fundamentally view change itself. You are asking the organization to "align with uncertainty" for the long run. *You are asking them to be "at arms" in mind and in action, all the time. You are proposing a never-ending march forward and asking them to be ready to transform on demand.*

Managing change in an organization once is hard. Demanding it over and over is significantly harder. Help employees see the importance of this need to constantly change, help them disrupt their obsolete tempos and outlooks. Facilitate a shift in their routines by fostering trust in leadership and in each other—if they believe in "why and how," they will change. Seeing the severity of problems and the vastness of opportunities will trigger their innate desire to evolve—don't focus on getting consensus on solutions; seek agreement around the need to change.

Just before the massive auto industry bailout in the U.S., GM leaders and all of their employees could clearly see the end. Their survival was in question. They had to act and change—leaving their past beliefs and arguments behind. The solutions were clear: better products, better service, and cost control. However, they had not realized the severity of the problem. Why change the comfortable routines if we don't have to? The economic collapse forced them to take swift actions to survive. In a fast moving world, dangers are always around the corner and it is only by acknowledging them and their consequences that we can focus on next steps.

Value the natural rhythm people have in their lives and at the company, recognize that they will not change that rhythm just because you say so. Help them fuel their natural urge to evolve; let them see the problems and the dangers and help them trust in you, in each other, and in the need to change. Individuals may be playing the game but teams beat the odds. Emergence is the pattern that an organization, a living entity, creates as a whole. Let them emerge as a team and as a unit.

—— CHAOS IS YOUR PLAYMATE ——

Alignment with uncertainty can lead to a perceived state of chaos. Challenges and opportunities will approach and unfold rapidly and sporadically. There will be an overload of problems, solutions, and options—a never-ending state of crisis.

Today, most organizations are designed to provide consistent and predictable results, not provoke crises. They are expected to prevent problems, they insist on controlling uncertainty. This is wrong; it is not valuable. A crisis mentality can be productive. You live in a chaotic non-linear competitive world. A world filled with crisis.

It is not easy to run a company that is always in crisis mode, but is not wise to let your competitors take advantage of the turbulence while you wait; embrace crisis, don't fight it. Work in short cycles of recognizing and/or instigating crisis followed by periods of stabilization (cool down) but don't get comfortable with a "steady as she goes" approach.

Oppenheimer & Team

Early in 1939, German physicists learned the secrets of splitting the uranium atom. Fear of unspeakable destruction by the Nazis broke out in America. President

Roosevelt was urged by U.S. scientists and military personnel to develop an atomic research program.

In late 1941, the American effort to design and build an atomic bomb began: the "Manhattan Project." The main facility was at Los Alamos, New Mexico.

Professor Robert Oppenheimer led the effort. The Manhattan Project was so secretive that supposedly even Vice-President Truman never heard of it until he became president, even though it employed over 120,000 workers and had cost nearly $2 billion by 1945. In competing with Nazis in the first nuclear arms race, many credit Oppenheimer and his approach to innovation as a key contributor to achieving results. Oppenheimer focused relentlessly on fostering a creative culture fueled by crisis. This environment emphasized winning and not allocating credit to individuals. Although some may question the morality of the results, no one can argue with the effectiveness of the process.

It is no secret that hugely successful companies like Google, Amazon, Tesla, Oracle, Apple, Microsoft, and many more have benefited from their cultures of innovation, which stems from fierce competition. They recognize individuals for contributions but teams for accomplishments. Measure and award around collective work and avoid a "Shamu" (the showcase whale) reward system—roll, jump, dance . . . every action gets a fish. Exciting work, innovative culture, collective evolution, and salary should be the primary reward for performance; extraordinary success and evolutionary accomplishments are never based on only one person's work.

To succeed, build a work environment that aligns with uncertainty and embraces crisis. To do this, create an atmosphere for the free exchange of intelligence, un-constrained by functions and turfs. Advocate a culture of critical thinking and transparency, and let the results be shared accomplishments. Help the organization view strategy and execution as a continuum, with no clear beginnings or endings. In this way, crisis is not so much a bad word as it is just another opportunity. Make crisis your playground and chaos your playmate.

Create an environment inspired by crisis. Let innovation and experimentation uncover the ways to turn crisis into competitive advantages, over and over. Allow people to imagine, innovate, and thrive across the organization. Walt Disney credited his company's and team's success to their "never-ending curiosity which keeps leading them down new paths."

"Against the ruin of the world,
there is only one defense: the creative act."
—Kenneth Rexroth, Poet

To every disadvantage there is a corresponding advantage. Fuel the creative act and find it!

ALIGN WITH UNCERTAINTY

Or risk never becoming a butterfly!

Recognize that you must change, always. Shed your fears and realize that change is good for you. Help your people desire to move from caterpillars to butterflies; lead them there.

Shift your mind, align with uncertainty, and live with probability.

Mission Beta: Capture and Interrogate Reality

Get real and stay real about your company, your capabilities, your performance and your markets. Make it achievable, always.

In late spring of 1999, I was invited to a private conference in Boca Raton, Florida. Lots of golfing, plenty of drinking and fancy food, and a few business presentations by the "who's who" of the first "Dot Com" onslaught, or the era of "Irrational Exuberance," according to the Federal Reserve Bank Chairman Alan Greenspan.

I attended a presentation by a senior executive of an early stage company, which focused on their strategy, the state of Internet, and the opportunities in E-commerce. I sat next to the CEO of a Fortune 500 retail company. About 15 to 20 minutes into the presentation, the room was pitch dark and silent; all eyes were on the map of the United States that covered the entire wall behind the presenter. Bright color arrows were connecting the states to icons representing massive warehouses (coming soon). With a click of the remote came more arrows with different colors, and then more, as the speaker discussed products and sourcing patterns. It was a wonder of colors and a masterful PowerPoint slide. The map looked like a master plan for an intercontinental nuclear ballistic missile attack.

At this point, the CEO next to me slowly turned and whispered, "What are these guys smoking?" He was right, the vision was inches short of insane.

During a break, that same CEO shared the challenges in his business—the need for people to touch and feel the goods ("no one will buy unless they see the product"), the complexities of merchandizing and supply chain management, and the art of living with thin margins. "You have to have physical stores and keep a lot of inventory . . . that is the way this business works," he insisted.

You may have heard of that early stage company with the overwhelming vision: "Amazon." They sold books, then other goods, then made books. Next they developed the Kindle to deliver books electronically and used the content markers to understand their customers' needs in order to sell more books and other goods. They figured out the complex distribution model and went from a "zero inventory" model to an "owned goods model." They figured out more responsive ways to keep stock, manage their warehouses, and ship goods—methods better suited to their internet-based business model. Along the way, they realized that all the technology and servers they owned could become a revenue-generating asset for them; they turned the additional server capacity (idle machines) into a separate and very lucrative business —the Amazon EC2 (Elastic Computer Cloud).

The EC2 provided computing power to smaller companies and entrepreneurs at a very affordable price and with a pay-as-you go model; you need a server, you get a server, you need it for a day, pay for a day or an hour, you need hundreds of machines, scale up with a few line of programming codes and get that. They created the first real commercially viable "cloud": computers available to use or rent, via Internet access. Amazon appreciated the reality of "extra server capacity" and the market needs for computers and flexibility, then combined the two trends all the way to the bank. They changed, and changed some more. They utterly adapted and evolved into something very different from what they were. And they're still doing it.

Amazon's vision presented in Florida was remarkable but their ability to stay real about their capabilities while aggressively pushing the envelope of innovation is a touchstone of achievement. Amazon never stopped having a "big" vision. They simply managed to keep it achievable by taking advantage of the market dynamics and opportunities while keeping within their realities of execution—they kept it achievable, always.

As for the retail CEO, he looked like a hero after the "Dot Com" bubble of 2000 burst. But he was forced to resign a few years later since his company was showing dismal financial results and limited promise of fighting the new market forces and competitors such as Amazon. He did not appreciate the reality of change around him and failed to evolve. On that day, in that conference room, he not only failed to recognize the butterfly before him, but he killed his own caterpillar.

Poor execution is often the result of a difference between reality (capabilities, performance, markets) and ill-considered ambition. In other words, always "keep it real".

No process, or person is ever 100% effective. No supply chain is truly risk-free. And no economic, political, and competitive environment stays the same. Strategies often fail because we base our decisions on what we "expect," as opposed to what "is" the reality.

To appreciate reality is to understand what your capabilities and performance actually are, to comprehend the changes and uncertainties in markets, customer needs, and innovations, and to realize the potential impact these have on your aspirations. Make sure that the assumptions that you and those surrounding you have made over the year do not become your false reality. Does your reality coincide with your plans?

Make it achievable. I speak of the obvious, because the obvious is often dangerously ignored.

Execution is a function of bringing all your capabilities into focus. Design your strategies with a sharp emphasis on the realities of your organization and the environment in which you compete. **This is how aspirations move from theoretical to achievable.**

Admitting you have a problem is the first step towards sobriety. It is also the first step of effective execution. Recognize your company's imperfections and be realistic about your goals. (The emperor can only clothe himself if he knows he has no clothes on!)

Let me be clear: not every strategy is for you. Constantly find where to play and how to win based on the realistic situation in front of you. Big visions are only worth having if they are made achievable.

—— PLAN TO IMPROVISE ——

To focus is important. To focus on the right item at the right time is critical. In fact, it is what separates the winners from the losers.

Experts may advise, "Have a firm conviction about your strategy and pursue it relentlessly." I disagree. Convictions can be deadly—the wrong convictions will waste your organization's energy and resources.

Over the years, I have reviewed thousands of business plans and worked with hundreds of entrepreneurs. I have yet to see a success story that is 100% based on the original plan. All seasoned generals know that "No battle plan survives contact with the enemy" and all experienced entrepreneurs know that plans must change as they face customers, employees, partners, technology, market, and competition.

> *"Everybody has a plan until they get punched in the face."*
>
> **—Mike Tyson,
> World Boxing Champion**

Four years before the introduction of personal computers, the CEO of Digital Equipment Corporation (DEC), Ken Olsen, said, "There is no reason anyone would want a computer in their home." The company maintained this belief through a downward spiral . . . until after 25 years on the fortune 500 list, DEC was sold in 1998.

History is a great teacher. Mistakes can be good, but repeated mistakes are sinful. Remember to capture the essence of the wave of change heading your way and to interrogate your reality to understand the gap between capabilities and desires.

In the mid to late 1990s, Kmart set out to compete with Walmart on price. Kmart stayed committed to this vision . . . until it filed for bankruptcy in 2002. The company failed to adjust their capabilities (mostly on supply-chain readiness) or to adjust their focus as Walmart had done.

In 1975, Eastman Kodak developed the first digital camera (even though these cameras did not become popular until the mid-1990s). However, Kodak executives did not pursue this market; they were committed to old products and an old approach, fearing a loss of their film stock business (which they lost anyway). Having missed the opportunity, the company filed for bankruptcy in 2012.

There is no monopoly on naïveté. Learn and apply, constantly. To win, you must operate with relentless and shifting focus. To do this, be aware of your capabilities, limitations, conflicting objectives, and consequences. In a dynamic and explosively competitive world, all is in flux, including your focus.

Timing and focus are critical—just as in surfing. Catch the wave too early and you're beaten down by its force. Paddle too late and it passes you by. In business be aware of timing in order to act and refocus advantageously. What's more, yesterday's focus is not necessarily the best focus for today or tomorrow. *In an uncertain environment, focus is never static. Be prepared to shift yours often.*

Martin Cooper -
father of the cellular phone

Marty Cooper, the father of cell phone technology shares a story about Motorola and AT&T. "In 1982, Bell systems was still building car telephones, even though at Motorola, we had demonstrated 'portables.' But AT&T [Bell] did not adjust its focus; they went to the biggest consultant they could find who went out and asked customers about the 'car phone' business. The customers talked about the kind of car telephones they liked and the usage level. AT&T concluded that the maximum market for car telephones in the next ten years was 900,000 units. And it turns out they were pretty close. That's about as many car telephones as were sold. But in the same ten years we sold millions of cell phones."

Customers can help you enhance products and improve services. They can stimulate your imagination and feed your curiosity. But innovation is hidden in the unknowns and is always a secret first. Peter Thiel, the founder of PayPal, in his book *Zero to One* writes that "every correct answer is necessarily a secret: something important and unknown, something hard to do but doable . . . the best place to look for secrets is where no one is looking." Remember, innovation is the gold hidden in the depth of unknowns and must be discovered.

The AT&T story is an instructive one. Having the right focus matters. Shifting your focus at the right time is also critical. Alignment with uncertainty sets the stage for shifting your focus. Awareness of the realities of your company (its capabilities and performance) provides the framework to keep your plans achievable. The irony is that years later Motorola led the cell phone market with the stylish Razr phones in 2006 (about $43 billion in sales) but failed to introduce new products and stayed committed to the old phone technologies until 2010 when, due to the iPhone and Blackberry, it saw a drop of 90% in stock value. Of course, today Blackberry is on its last legs, proving that no one has exclusive rights to inflexibility and being blind to change.

First Uber chooses to be in the transportation business instead of selling routing and fare management software, then it goes from running a taxi-like business to being in water transportation (private ferries) and then on to delivering groceries. Amazon figures that there is money in delivery (paying a considerable amount to other providers for free shipping on products sold on its site) and aims to deploy delivery drones and employ an army of drivers; moves that Uber, UPS, and Fed-Ex should watch very closely. AirBnB is exploring new frontiers to compete with its recent move to acquire Lapka, a device company that monitors home and office environments. It is experimenting with a new focus and aiming to leverage the relationships it has with people and homes to enter the lucrative Internet of Things market.

Constantly looking for the right focus at the right time is the path to staying relevant and the road to sustainable victory.

———————

Bring change and reality together constantly. Pair your strategies with your realities (cash, people, talents, partners, intellectual property, manufacturing, and distribution). Focus on the advantages that provide the best chance to win. And then refocus again as new challenges and opportunities arise.

Whether you acknowledge it or not, the fact is that all advantages are temporary and all plans are provisional. But your resolve to win must be unequivocal and permanent. No plan is perfect and none is lasting. At all times, remain flexible to choose the most likely path to win. ***Be prepared to improvise—plan on it.***

Planning to improvise is not about winging it when faced with a mighty opponent or a failing strategy. A winning strategy is adaptable from the start. Make your plans fungible. Be ready to improvise quickly, but not abruptly. Anticipate the need to improvise by creating a menu of strategies, a portfolio of complementary schemes (as opposed to a highly customized plan for a single and narrow advantage). Then execute in waves and pivot as needed.

"In preparing for battle I have always found that plans are useless, but planning is indispensable."

—Dwight D. Eisenhower,
U.S. President

How quickly your company can shift focus and pivot is a function of how dynamic your organization is. If you're agile in planning but not in doing, the most compelling competitive advantages may get away from you. And there is no advantage to executing an obsolete plan with great speed either!

——— CREATE A NEW REALITY ———

Don't be handcuffed by your realities. You can be a butterfly. You can evolve over and over.

The larval stage of a caterpillar (the juvenile period before adulthood) is all about growth. Within the span of a few weeks, the caterpillar will grow exponentially to over a thousand times its mass and go through many definable phases of change, before building the cocoon and positioning herself to become a butterfly. Making it real is not equal to making it confined and limiting your capabilities. It is about maximizing what you can accomplish at each stage of your existence and then recognizing when you are ready for the next stage of evolution.

By all accounts, Google has been a tremendous success from the days it was conceived as a university project in 1995 to twenty years later in 2015, from being an online search company to a new age advertising platform. It then became a video and cell phone platform with YouTube and Android. It went from indexing and organizing information on the web to an email and online application (Gmail, Google Docs, Sheets, Slides, and more) provider; from guiding us through traffic with Google Maps to capturing the earth through Google Earth.

And then . . . Alphabet is born! Investors are happy with a big immediate bump in stock prices and Wall Street is delighted because it can get better visibility into the financials of Google without the noise of other investments and experimental divisions. By making Google, Fiber, Nest, Calico, Google X, Google Life Sciences, and Google Ventures independent companies under the newly created shell "Alphabet" (Url: ABC.XYZ), Google executives created a new reality.

In response to Wall Street criticism of too much

experimentation and lack of visibility in operating costs, Google could have scaled down investments or stopped pushing the envelope with new "out of the box" ideas. But they did the opposite, they gave Wall Street what it wanted while fueling all the other Google divisions with an entrepreneurial boost. Perhaps they figured out that they had become too big to innovate, and too diverse to maintain focus and accountability.

In an open letter to the public and investors announcing the creation of Alphabet, Larry Page wrote "We did a lot of things that seemed crazy at the time. Many of those crazy things now have over a billion users, like Google Maps, YouTube, Chrome, and Android . . . . Companies tend to get comfortable doing the same thing, just making incremental changes . . . where revolutionary ideas drive the next big growth areas, you need to be a bit uncomfortable to stay relevant."

Always changing, always evolving; that is the way Alphabet (formerly Google) has provided above market returns to investors, year after year.

If you don't alter your capabilities or performance to realize a competitive advantage, you may not be thinking big enough. Remember, to appreciate reality is not to be constrained by it. Be aware of your realities and be prepared to improve them. <u>Using concrete steps, innovate your way out of a disadvantageous position.</u>

Bob Kleist started his business (Printronix) in his garage and struggled to get investor funding for years. He spotted a true market need, persisted, and then succeeded. Bob is an inventor (a pioneer in printer technology), an entrepreneur, and a talented board member, who took his company public. He had the courage to evolve himself and his company many times over to secure victory after victory.

When asked about dealing with today's fast moving competition, Bob proposed, "There are two major trends in the marketplace today. One is technology—it is changing at an increasingly rapid rate and every technology either becomes obsolete or a commodity. At the same time, you have a global economic and competitive situation that is changing very vigorously; so if you want to have a successful company, you've got to catch both of these waves . . . at the same time. Once you understand the opportunities and changing needs, you need to assess your ability to meet them. Do you have the capabilities? If not, what is missing? And what is the timing? If you made this change, how long would it take? And what kind of investment would you have to make? Can you accomplish this on your own or should you partner or acquire someone?" Bob's advice is to "understand your capabilities, look at improving them, and then adjust your strategies."

Aim to get to your improved reality in lockstep with your strategy. Don't get too far ahead of yourself or else your plan will collapse; but don't alter your realities too quickly in anticipation of a plan either, or else you may be satisfying the needs of an obsolete strategy. In other words, don't build capabilities too far ahead of the need dictated by your strategy, otherwise you may be building the wrong competencies. Control your excitement about the long-term possibilities and the complex corporate transformation process ahead of you.

A few years back I invested in a company involved in sports analytics and intelligence. The company had great technology for that time and was packed with promise of upside. They simulated sports games like football, soccer, and baseball and, with a really high probability, could pick the winners and losers. At the beginning, they built a nice and steady subscription-based business. We had a board meeting every month and almost every month management presented a new strategy for growth—despite the board's direction to keep focus on the subscription business and to innovate around their strength and momentum.

Management, which had controlling interest, was fascinated with big swings. They constantly pursued complex relationships with giant media companies and built products and capabilities to fulfill the needs of their grandiose dreams. In the process, they wasted considerable capital and slowly missed the market opportunities in their base business. They tried to transform the business model, the customer base, and the value propositions over and over, while refusing to acknowledge the realities of market and resources. Along the way management team blocked a viable acquisition offer and some distribution partnerships.

When entertainment and gaming became the new flavor of corporate growth, I resigned from the board and insisted that they get a couple of game experts on the board and management team, raise additional capital dedicated to this effort, and focus like hell for once! They aimed to build a platform capable of serving millions of players simultaneously, before even a single game was proven valuable to customers. More money was wasted in building unnecessary capabilities. After a couple of more years, the board had enough votes to change management.

Around 2012, the company was sold essentially for assets and most of us lost our investment. The management continued to confuse distraction with innovation and chased the market in a series of fruitless transformational activities.

I learned to be less patient, more vocal, and a bit harsher after this experience.

Be conscious of time and uncertainty. As you dabble with flavor-of-the-day strategies and fail to execute, markets, advantages, and opportunities are passing you by. Randomly changing the drugs and the treatment in hopes of gaining your health is nothing short of gambling with your life. Alternatively, as you methodically pursue your multi-year transformation efforts, the market is shifting, new competitors are surfacing, technology is renewing, and customer needs are evolving. By the time you transform, the advantage you wanted may be long gone. Delivering even a miraculous cure to the patient, after she is dead, is not victory!

The point is ***Appreciate Reality:*** yours, and the market's. *Or risk extinction.*

Assess achievability constantly and without bias. Be prepared to shift your focus, at all times. Innovate, and break the barriers of your realities. Bet on advantages being temporary. Keep your aims and plans fungible. Plan to improvise, seek more "Ahas," and be ready to excel.

—— MISSION GAMMA— REACH FOR MORE ——

Expand your universe of possibilities by becoming more curious. Admit that there may be opportunities and challenges yet unknown and actively seek them. Aspire for more.

"Would you tell me, please,
which way I ought to go from here?"
"That depends a good deal on where you want to get to,"
said the Cat.
"I don't much care where—" said Alice.
"Then it doesn't matter which way you go," said the Cat.
"So long as I get SOMEWHERE,"
Alice added as an explanation.

"Oh, you're sure to do that," said the Cat,
"if you only walk long enough."

—Lewis Carroll
Alice in Wonderland

The key to getting to an "Aha" is ***purposeful curiosity***. The kind of discovery that is tenacious and expansive, but directed. Curiosity is purposeful when it produces positive results consistently, building a path to more "Ahas." Become inquisitive and discover more.

The most common causes of strategic failure are solving the wrong problem, or pursuing the wrong opportunity. But the right opportunities are not served on a silver platter—they need to be discovered. Today's business "reality show" does not occur in a fantasy land, and unlike Alice in Wonderland, you don't have "time to walk long enough." No one will give you directions to the next competitive advantage.

When looking for competitive advantages of tomorrow, a 2014 McKinsey survey suggests that eight out of ten times, strategists focus on known hypotheses— opportunities that have been examined in the past or are already evident (i.e., generals are always fighting the last war).

Discovery means constant observation of realities and uncertainties, and endless scrutiny of data and signals. It is finding competitive advantages and shaping strategies more rigorously (both from the top down and the bottom up).

The discovery path can cut in any given direction. Killer advantages won't come to you—go out and find them! Here is a clue . . . use data.

DIAMONDS ONLY SHINE IN THE LIGHTS

The best way to find advantage and inform strategies is through data analytics. Although every good executive knows this fact, in the interest of expediency or to avoid egocentric conflicts, many ignore it. Make data your friend, embrace it. Let it shed light on situations and be the beacon for discovery. Data speaks the truth if you're willing to listen. It is the ultimate objective criteria, the very best argument. Edward Deming, proclaims that only God should be trusted without data and all others should make their case based on data and analysis. Some suggest that even God is presenting his case through the data offered by nature.

But having data does not equal having a good plan. You can have the best race car, built for success, but winning a NASCAR race needs excellent driving too. Data does not strategize and find the advantage, you do.

Again from Marty Cooper, "I learned an important lesson early in my career—you may have all the right tools, but unless there is commitment to use them, an openness to embrace outcomes, and to do it continuously, they are useless."

Remember, it is not about technology or tools, it is about speed, approach, and commitment. It is about unmasking uncertainty to understand the dangers ahead and finding the diamonds (advantages) in the mine faster than the competition. But caution is in order; remember that if tortured and twisted, data will tell you whatever you want—don't justify your decision with data; instead, use it to find the path to the next advantage. Then commit to your decision, but only until it is time to pivot once again.

Several years ago, I partnered with two investor-friends to acquire a niche company through a "carve-out" (buying a piece of a bigger company). We devised a growth strategy centered on the use of data analytics. The company was involved in global distribution of electronic components—a tough, fast moving, and cut-throat business. We grew the revenues by thirty fold in less than three years while maintaining great bottom line results. Data was aggregated from thousands of vendors and customers. The aim was to leverage the disparity between supply and demand in order to win. Analytics drove our purchasing, our pricing, our sales incentive patterns, and our entire strategy. It took time, but we earned our workers' trust for the controversial decisions we made based on data and analytics. The strategy worked and we proved it with profits.

We aggregated product availability and pricing on over 10,000 specific parts ranging from Memory to Diodes to Transistors. We constantly analyzed the buying patterns across

*the globe. Every morning in California our sales team received
(on their computers) a list of part numbers and clients coupled
with pricing and quantities to offer—call "xyz" company, offer
"ABC" part at $x. The process started again as our Hong Kong
office opened and then the baton was passed to our London office.
The end result was a whopping 60% to 70%+ closing ratio (close
to 5x to 7x higher than average for the industry). Our objective
was to balance the risk and the return and manage a portfolio of
opportunities and increase customer re-purchase rates. Decisions
were not only based on individual transactions and margins,
but also on portfolio risk and client value metrics. We aimed to
turn our capital as often as possible. Our product concentration
strategy would shift almost on a daily basis and the composition
of the inventory and our return expectations would follow.*

*Unfortunately, after some of us left the company, the
new leaders let the old habits of "chasing margins" settle right
back in—the result was a 90% drop in revenue. Our wins
were a direct function of having the most comprehensive view of
market movements possible, constantly mapping opportunities
against our financial and performance capabilities, turning
data into actionable insights fast, and last but not least, having
management and employees that trusted the analytics enough to
bet their careers on it. Without all this, the company entered a
death spiral.*

Use data analytics to instill trust by confirming
that the organization is fighting the right battle. Use it to

discover challenges and opportunities and to demonstrate the seriousness of the need to change. Let data analytics constantly deliver the signals, news, and insights—pointing out both direction and progress. Let it inform you of the uncertain path ahead and how to best manage it in order to win. Let it constantly help you discover the imperfections of your realities and measure the impacts of planned future actions. Let it help you spot the best timing for a pivot.

—— SEIZE THE EXCITEMENT ——

More data leads directly to more opportunities for discovery. But it can also lead to confusion—trying to process too much data can choke a company.

To harness this bottomless and ever expanding source of information effectively, methodically, and continually, is to gain a significant and perpetual competitive advantage. Remember, data is your friend . . . perhaps your best friend. Learn to trust it, but never forget to verify it. To start, don't look at data (big or small) as a byproduct. View it as a critical asset, a depository of intelligence for today, tomorrow, and every day. See it as your competitive weapon.

In 1978, at 39 years old, Don Beall led one of the largest aerospace and defense companies in the world, Rockwell International. He was one of the youngest and most powerful Fortune 500 CEOs.

Under Don's leadership, Rockwell doubled its revenue to nearly $12 billion. His focus on cutting-edge technologies and managerial leadership was exemplified in aerospace programs such as the Space Shuttle, the B-1 Bomber, GPS satellites, ICBM, and nuclear submarine precision navigation systems. Don led a giant defense and technology company in one of the most uncertain times of recent history (the Cold War era) and guided its evolution and growth.

Don, a former CEO of a complex and global enterprise who also sat on the boards of iconic companies like Procter and Gamble, Amoco and Time Warner told me, "If companies are more dynamic, key assumptions and strategies can be monitored, almost in real time. With today's data availability you can adjust as you fly . . . and that kind of proposition is very exciting . . . I wish we had that when I was leading Rockwell."

Make this excitement yours and seize the opportunity. Make data your "on time' truth teller. Make analytics help you discover and create focus. But don't expect analytics to replace people's intelligence and perspective. Don't over complicate analytics and don't attempt to boil the ocean by trying to overload analysis with too much data.

Discovery only results from linking facts, patterns, and probabilities through critical thinking and unbiased judgment of data. It arises out of relating hindsight (what we know from the past), insight (what we discern about today) and foresight (what we expect in the future). Data is the critical ingredient, analysis purifies and provides context, and then critical thinking sheds light on the advantage.

Paul Slack, a Marine Brigadier General who was responsible for a $2.4 billion budget before he retired, says that, "The key is intelligence and communications.

Having timely intelligence and the ability to communicate are probably the two things that give us the leg up in a mission; it is about turning data in to an advantage fast. Today, the basic infantry man has got more communications at his fingertips than we probably had at a regimental level. The challenge is to be able to use it wisely."

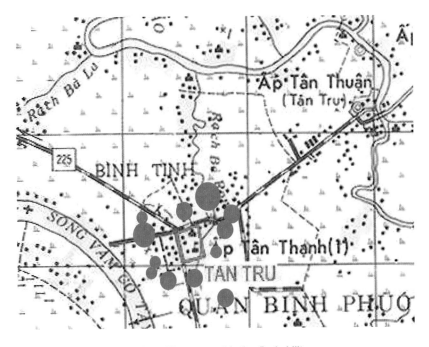

Red Dots, Vietnam, and Action Probability

Paul shares a valuable example, "When I was a young major in the Marine Corps, fighting in Vietnam, we did not school-train our intelligence officers at the lower levels. It was the last lieutenant out of the field who became an Intel officer. He could tell me if it was raining or not, but I got no real information, nothing about our reality on the ground. Finally, I told him to go out into the villages in the district headquarters. And every time he hears something that sounds unusual, like people in the wrong place or some village that got attacked in the night, to put a red dot on a map. And I asked him to do it every day. At the end of a short period of time I had a cluster, a little cluster of red dots . . . that is where we're going to operate, that is where the action is . . . We should look at every mission in terms of probabilities. Here's a cluster of red dots, obviously tells me that there is a higher likelihood that the action is there."

"Insight" is an offspring of the partnership between data and purposefully curious leaders and employees. Data alone is a series of "1s" and "0s." When combined with human ability to change the frame of reference and triangulate with experience and other data it turns to knowledge. Paul only promotes the same idea that Plato did over 2300 years ago: a good decision is based on knowledge and not just numbers.

Paul's story underscores that it is not about making something overly complex. It is about discovering the signals that really matter, turning that data into intelligence quickly, and then winning the war one battle at a time.

"Aha" resides in data: discover it, and then measure the advantages it offers through analytics. Data flows constantly and carries the gift of intelligence. Reach for more. Look for new "Ahas," always. Never forget to change your frame of reference to learn more. Consider the exchange of value between the organization and its stakeholders and be aware of the impact of signals on growth, risk, and efficiency.

BE EXERTIVE

Permanent and absolute wins in the business world are marvels of the past. Realize that success is never final and failure is fatal only if it is understood too late and not learned from. The world may be in flux and uncertain, but every moment could be the instant the solution to a problem becomes clear—the "Aha" moment. Be exertive. Turn the table, make "Aha" not just a moment of sudden insight, but demand and expect "Ahas" with every breath you take—plan for them and plan for your next evolution!

Endlessly craving for and discovering "Ahas" are demanding challenges. Executing against an ever evolving plan, mobilizing the resources, constantly correcting course, and realizing the advantages in the marketplace are also tough challenges. There is a vast chasm between desire and outcome, which must be crossed before you can evolve and thrive. The competitive world of tomorrow is "**Do or Die**," to succeed you must understand and overcome the natural frictions.

"What is dangerous is not to evolve."

**—Jeff Bezos,
Founder and CEO Amazon**

——— NOT SO COMMON ——— AND NOT SO SIMPLE

As individuals, we strategize every day: we consider the route and the probability of the normal traffic and accidents; we examine the time available for the travel; the fuel we require; and the status of our vehicle. We may even consider the options of ride sharing or working from home. At the origin, and along the way, we consult the traffic news on the radio, Google Maps, or Waze, to monitor traffic and possible reroutes. We check our speed against the posted signs constantly. In our simplest daily activity we consider our resources, explore alternatives, impose time, consider relevance, predict outcomes, and adjust course . . . we use "common sense" and analytics. Coleridge, the poet, suggests that wise person is he who enjoys an uncommon degree of common sense. Be wise.

To match the speed and complexity of the competitive

world and to devise plans and actions that increase the odds of winning, strategic thinking is a must, and analytics capabilities are critical. But the value of common sense (that not so common commodity) should not be dismissed.

If a strategy does not pass the test of common sense, you should re-think, re-calibrate, and re- strategize. The most brilliant strategies and successful executions are simple, understandable, and "make sense."

Common sense is not so common and simplicity is not so simple.

The world is complex, fast, and uncertain. The simple answer is the best answer because simplicity can be grasped faster and understood better. To align with uncertainly and appreciate reality and to aim for a constant flow of "Ahas," your strategies and definition of success must be clearly communicated, and the battle grounds must be well targeted, as you march for a new advantage. At all times be careful of what George Bernard Shaw calls the single biggest problem in communication: the illusion that it has taken place.

Simplify your strategies, actions, and the way you monitor progress. Plans and directions that are complex or misunderstood lead to delayed and confused results. Worse, they lead to poor outcomes and lost opportunities.

Keeping it simple means shaping cogent plans and communicating them clearly. Clarity of communication is at the heart of every well-conceived and executed strategy, dynamic or otherwise. Clarity is paramount to good execution and timely course correction. Big words and complicated objectives do not produce superior results. Just the opposite.

Leonardo da Vinci viewed simplicity as "the ultimate sophistication." Albert Einstein proclaimed, "Any intelligent fool can make things bigger and more complex, but it takes a touch of genius with a lot of courage to seek simplicity."

The point is—*be sophisticated, be a genius, be courageous . . . aim for simplicity.*

ASPIRE FOR MORE

And prepare to fly

Take advantage of "Ahas" with speed and confidence.

Remain curious and let data and analytics be the beacon that guides you to your next advantage. Continuous exertion, not just the plan, nor insights, technology, and tactics improves your odds of winning.

Dreams can be real if pursued with courage. Don't leave change to chance. Missions can be accomplished if approached with passion and conviction.

Emergence begins with desire. Gain the caterpillar's edge, plan to be a butterfly. Evolve, evolve again, and thrive in business.

---

*"Those who do not move,
do not notice their chains."*

—Rosa Luxemburg

PART FOUR

DO OR DIE...
EVOLVE AND THRIVE

*First they ignore you,
then they laugh at you,
then they fight you,
then you win.*

—Mahatma Gandhi

CHAPTER 7
GET YOUR HEAD OUT
OF THE BOAT

Gregor Samsa woke up one morning from a disturbing dream. He found himself changed into a grotesque cockroach; on his back and stiff with monstrous looking arch-shaped ribs, and multiple tiny legs. Kafka's hapless protagonist has experienced a metamorphosis. Leaders and companies can also wake up one morning and see themselves transformed into an inferior and immobile entity; beginning their journey toward a demise. *Positive evolutions are purposeful, intelligent, and planned.*

———— DON'T LEAVE CHANGE ————
TO CHANCE

"Get your head out of the boat" is a reminder to sailors that they need to pay attention to more than sail trim and the various instruments showing boat speed, compass heading, etc. Go beyond the analysis of facts and numbers to focus on what is actually behind the progress (or regress). Learn to measure the strategy and not necessarily the outcome. Once you get your head out of the boat, you can win in a future where disruption is an expected norm, and all people and things are connected.

Recognize that friction is natural. We have tried it before, we are too big or too small, and our business is just different. We are the dominant player with a lot of cash or an early stage company with limited funding. We don't have the right technology, people, culture, data, leadership team, customers, and sales channels. These are all good excuses not to change. But they are also excellent reasons to evolve.

You are not making a change if you are not facing an opposition. The laws of physics make friction the counter force. Shifting your mind and actions to win is no different. The defenders of the status quo offer common pushbacks. Some naysayers are adamant that strategy cannot be dynamic: we cannot change our focus constantly and execution requires consensus building and time. Others push back because they don't see the need to change and the urgency to evolve: we are the market leader, we have been doing this for a long time and know the industry, we have a complex supply chain, our brand is trusted and we have a cost advantage, etc. In other words, we are "It" and our past success is the proof. There is no need to panic, strategize more rapidly or change—we have the advantage and we are sustaining it! The opposition (or the addicted, the fearful of change, those comfortable with the way things are—however you wish to brand them) can invent a million obstacles to transformation.

Friction is the unavoidable side effect of the fear of change. Change is the law of life and inevitable. Your job is to push through the frictions, overcome the fears and embrace its constant nature. You must not leave change to chance.

"Everything you've ever wanted
is on the other side of fear."

—George Addair,
newspaperman & real estate mogul,

———————

Frictions aside, there are real challenges to overcome: the size of the organization, the complexity and nature of the business, and the characteristics of the data available. There are conflicts to resolve, positions to take, and positions to change. If there are no problems, there is no progress; worthy advantages come with issues that are worth confronting. You will never discover the new frontiers and life changing advantages unless you have the courage to lose sight of the coastline, weather the storms, and make the wind your friend.

There are two primary choices in life: accept conditions as they exist, or accept the responsibility for changing them (Walt Disney); It is no use saying 'we are doing our best', you have to do what is necessary (Winston Churchill). Take the responsibility and make the choice of leaving the comfortable shores and the safety of land. The ship maybe safe at harbor, but that is not what ships are built for (John A. Shedd). You are built to evolve.

The caterpillar does not become a butterfly overnight. But its journey begins in an instant. A butterfly goes through four key stages in her lifecycle. The first stage is an egg. When the egg hatches the butterfly larva, the caterpillar, emerges. Then and only when caterpillar knows she is ready, she enters the next stage by transforming into a pupa and growing a hard shell. She manages to grow out of that shell (molts) by constructing new ones over and over (4 to 5 times). Along the way, the caterpillar adjusts to her environment by changing her color and shape. She protects herself with her poisonous safeguards and partners with others (e.g. ants). A purposeful evolution and process that could take as little as 3 weeks or for some (woolly bear caterpillars) as long as 14 years. An evolution from a crawling creature to an entirely different being that can fly, a butterfly—a purposeful metamorphosis. At every stage, the caterpillar faces challenges and frictions. She overcomes eminent dangers and turns her old self into her better version. Evolution, progress and change comes with friction and peril. Metamorphosis requires an unwavering commitment to tomorrow. To realize an improved future you must purposefully leave the past behind, and embrace the uncertainty ahead—constantly and without fear. You must evolve, then evolve again and thrive.

BUT, HOW?

Find the distinctive actions that stimulates your unique emergence. Like humans' 23 pairs of unique chromosomes (the defining DNA), every organization enjoys a one of a kind DNA—a genetic exclusivity that defines a unique path for emergence. Although certain actions and circumstances stimulate the emergence, the choice to react and to evolve is unique to each entity. There are actionable "hows" that can help accelerate, but do not guarantee, your transformation.

At school, in business, and in life we are trained to follow procedures—a series of activities based on a well-defined "how to" guide. We are assured that if we follow the process step by step, we will succeed. For the journey ahead, however, there are no structured procedures or guide books. There are only a series of stimuli with which to instigate your very own change and metamorphosis. At the end of the day, your evolution and patterns of emergence are unique to you and your organization; so is the process you choose and the actions you take.

The following concentration areas are neither procedures nor the single path to success—***they are ideas to inspire your change***:

1. Strategic recommendations should be made based on defensible probabilistic scenarios (quantify your decisions and the path you take for making those decisions)—no more conservative, optimistic and likely options.

2. Every plan has to offer a wave of strategies—a collection of related strategies with identifiable pivot points; demand to see the signals that will be monitored to trigger a pivot.

3. Avoid having independent plans by functions or business units—all plans must include internal and external shared signals that glue the organization together.

4. Shift from a consensus budget allocation to a zero-one mentality (different from zero based)—if an advantage is worthy of pursuit then pursue it with all your might. Don't dabble!

5. First fund to experiment and not to scale, then fund to win—that means don't waste time in figuring out how you scale before you have measured value, and don't hesitate when ready.

6. Business units and functions / departments must always plan for at least one innovation that is not incremental—they must i) identify and articulate the orthodoxies, ii) innovate by breaking them and iii) defend decisions with data.

7. Demand that all analysis must always offer multiple views of the problem or the opportunity—force the organization to always look at issues from various angles (by changing their frame of reference) and backing up their insights with data.

1. View and leverage "data" as an asset—not a byproduct of your execution and a means to measure your past actions. Declare that data and analytics will be driving decisions; then actually let it.

2. Always remember, it is about the problem not the solution—about the questions not the answers. Don't start with finding what you want—having a specific end in mind assumes the knowledge of the future; end goals will shift.

3. Control your urges to solve first and justify with data later. To gain new insight, always look to disprove yourself. Allow your conventional assumptions to be challenged.

4. Avoid getting a filtered view of the world—too much automated analytics results in ignoring new issues and rehashing the opportunities and problems framed up in the past.

5. Be a Hog (a data hog), a Cheetah (quick, calculating, and able to switch directions on the fly), and an Eagle (aware of minute details but capable of seeing the big picture).

6. You are the "business scientist," but get comfortable with data, analytics, and data scientists. You can delegate the technology infrastructure issues and decisions to the CTO / CIO, or data gathering and cleansing matters to the new chief data officers but don't delegate your strategy role.

7. You don't need to be exhaustive in capturing all signals first—there is a tomorrow! Start NOW, capture and evaluate signals and their changes from a growth, risk and efficiency perspective. Be constantly aware of the impact of value exchange between stakeholders. Don't get lost in the weeds, but don't position yourself to miss hidden insights either.

1. Don't aim to empower people. Aim to unleash the inherent abilities people bring to the organization—the power of imagination, action, and innovation. Let people belong and help drive your emergence.

2. Declare that failure is no longer toxic—make it safe to experiment. Create accountability around the ability to embrace flux and emerge —don't reward conformity

3. Erase the line between planning and execution. Be upfront with the organization: you will change the plan when needed; the month of the year is not going to dictate your destiny and the ability to gain a timely advantage.

4. Democratize data and analytics results—let data build the case for change and increase trust in management.

5. Measure three ways: BI, PI, and SI. The old fashion BI (Business Intelligence) - to describe and diagnose past performance. The new PI (Predictive Intelligence), dashboard of tomorrow—to anticipate outcomes if current trends continue. Finally, Strategic Intelligence (SI)— to monitoring success / failure of a wave of strategies, to explore scenarios based on probabilistic signals and to recognize pivot points.

6. Embrace a multi speed/multi scope approach to technology implementation initiatives. No more "do it" once, "do it" right approach. Aim for the "new" right, always.

7. Dynamic is different for every organization. Choose your initial pace and aim to beat it. Remember: being dynamic in planning and execution is different than being agile in executing against a static strategy.

> *"Chain of habits are too weak to be felt until they are too strong."*
>
> **—Warren Buffet**

The caterpillar evolves because it is in her nature to do so. She is not chained to her past. As she evolves from Larva to Pupa to Butterfly, she leaves her past behind—she makes her old self obsolete. She is able to survive while focusing on evolving. She builds her own future and is not satisfied with just enhancing her day to day performance (e.g. eating, crawling, etc.)

A human has 629 muscles. In contrast, a caterpillar has over 4,000 muscles, in a considerably smaller body.. The caterpillar uses every muscle to position herself for evolution, and employs her 12 eyes to distinguish the shades of gray—signals to understand her surroundings. She destroys her own shell (eats it) in order to grow and is not married to any state of her existence. She is committed to evolution: she trusts her instincts and uses every capability she has to destroy her past as she creates her future.

Trust the collection of your experiences, the data points you have captured over the years, and the resulting knowledge (your gut). But also trust that your "gut" can be enhanced; elevate your intuition with data, analysis and new intelligence, always. Seek those "Aha" moments that guide you to your next advantage by looking for anomalies and variations from the norm, watching for trends, examining the common beliefs, and realizing the frustrations. Learn from extremities, stagnations, and changes in momentum. These are the means of discovering insights.

Replace your habits with a constant drive for "Ahas", the new addiction. Don't confuse efforts with results and great performance with great strategy—measure both strategy and performance. Don't prescribe based on the past. Don't start with expecting what you want first—making the wrong decision first is not a good way to go! Quantify uncertainty and place your bets. Stay curious, let it help you discover, innovate, and stay relevant. Read the signals and pivot without hesitation. Keep in mind that "all insights are actionable"—if you choose to take action. Make it safe to experiment. Fire yourself and hire the new unbiased you. Put the force of data, analytics, and constant insights behind your strategies and actions.

Be forewarned, tomorrow is filled with more challenges and even more opportunities.

———

"Be great in act, as you have been in thought."

—William Shakespeare

———

CHAPTER 8
TWO MINUTE WARNING

"The future ain't what it used to be."

—Yogi Berra

In the NFL, the "Two Minute Warning" signals the end of a battle. It is the last chance to win. A short time before victory or defeat. A warning to the teams to step up and give it their all.

In spring of 1964, President Lyndon Johnson, was given a real life "Two Minute Warning." An ad-hoc commission delivered a report on forces that will soon re-shape the society and the economy: Civil Rights, Nuclear Weapons, and widespread Job Automation. While two out of three warnings created change, automation did not cause massive unemployment and social upheaval.

Similarly today, concerns around Automation, Artificial Intelligence, and Robotics are front and center. Experts have issued another imminent warning.

—— THE PATH AND THE UPSIDE ——

In 1950's Alan Turing first envisioned a machine that could think. Later John McCarthy from MIT coined the phrase "Artificial Intelligence" or AI. In the mid-1960's, Professor Joseph Weizenbaum created one of the first AI programs to simulate a virtual doctor. By 1984, investments from venture players and government dried up and progress in the field of AI slowed down (a stagnation period some refer to as the AI winter). Starting in the mid-1990's, as the potential for real financial return was discovered and computing capacity increased, AI progress built up some speed.

Today, various sources suggest that by 2025 the advent of AI, digital labor (replacing people with machines) and cognitive computing will impact close to 240 million knowledge workers. It will cause the elimination of a significant number of jobs and generate $6 trillion dollars of productivity gain. A Bank of America Merrill Lynch report predicted that by 2025 the "the annual creative disruption impact" from AI could range from $14 to $33 trillion, including $9 trillion of labor cost savings, $8 trillion of cost reduction in manufacturing and $2 trillion gains from deployment of self-driving cars and drones. To put these amounts in context, the GDP in 2016 is estimated at around $18 trillion. This level of efficiency upside is promising a $150 billion plus market for robots and AI with an estimated (by

London School of Economics) 600% to 800% return on investment for certain tasks; an attractive economic story offering a tsunami of business opportunities. This compelling value proposition has by some accounts caused a 4 to 10 times plus increase in the AI related investments since 2010 (from slightly north of $1.5 billion to estimated $8.5 to close to $20 billion—different sources).

The financial return opportunities and the productivity upsides are simply tremendous. However, it is unclear as to what future industries can generate tens of millions of new jobs to replace the ones under attack. Additionally, to realize the estimated returns, machines must be built to learn, to decide, and to evolve —or put simply, to take control. This anticipated loss of jobs and dominance of machines has triggered concerns.

THE DOWNSIDE: DEFEAT, EXTINCTION AND MAYHEM

In a recent controversial Oxford University report, automation was identified as a major displacement factor in workforce globally—impacting close to 50% of existing knowledge workers, or over 100 million people. Additionally, the anxiety of massive job loss is magnified by the fear of machine mastery; the idea that one day computers could become aware of themselves and build machines that are even more intelligent than humans. A creation effect that will increase the pace of dominance and eventually move the intelligence of machines beyond human comprehension—a hypothetical event called Singularity. This state will offer numerous moral and ethical challenges: Do machines have the same rights as men do? Should they get paid or qualify for time off? Would they be considered super knowledge workers and deserve more pay? Can machines get married, get life insurance, reproduce, die, and have an inheritance?

Artificial Intelligence is probably our biggest existential threat, Elon Musk claims. He warns that with AI we are summoning the demon, and that humans are close to taking the lid off something that could cause problems. Steve Wozniak, Bill Gates, and Stephen Hawking also advise caution. The head of IT at John Lewis (the major retail player in Europe) believes that rogue AI married to Internet of Things advancements "could signal the end of civilization." Ya Quin Zhang (president of the Chinese search engine giant Bidu) worries that as machines get smarter, people will in some ways become less smart; he fears that we might squander and get lost in this new mind space.

These alarming ideas from respectable thought leaders raises the question: should we give in to the fear and stop the evolution of machines, before it is too late?

161

AN ALTERNATIVE VIEW

Some experts remain skeptical of this very dark and dismal view of machine mastery, vast unemployment, and chaos. Peter Thiel, founder of PayPal, thinks that robots won't threaten the middle class jobs for at least a 100 years. Marc Andreessen, the respected venture capitalist, has been quoted to say "all this anxiety about robots eating the jobs will prove to have been a fever dream." Amazon has over 1000 people working on AI projects. Jeff Bezos acknowledges that AI is a big deal and states that "it is hard to overstate how big of an impact it's going to have on society over the next 20 years . . . while computers are getting smarter, their brain power is nowhere near as efficient as humans." This indicates that there is plenty of room to improve and evolve for decades to come, without a sense of immediate danger.

In a recent *Harvard Business Review* article, Thomas Davenport and Julia Kirby indicate that in the 21st century era, machines will take decisions away from humans. They suggest that "as machines encroach on decision making, it is hard to see the higher ground to which humans might move." However, they also believe that we should not necessarily view work as a zero-sum game with humans losing and machines gaining more and more share.

In other words, we can fear the inevitable, or choose to shape our relationship with machines differently. Let's view the partnership with machines as an opportunity to increase the size of the "pie"—expand the value delivered to humans and the society.

Machines learn from our experience and behavior. They learn by observing, tracing sequences, and mapping circumstances to actions. Machines learn within the framework of our orthodoxies and therefore act and react within the boundaries of our past beliefs and behaviors. Artificial Intelligence may offer solutions and actions based on what it has learned. But they cannot envision what has never before existed, or understood. Machines could not imagine that cars would displace horses. Computers can master deductive reasoning. They can, and will offer incremental enhancement— faster performance, better quality, improved speed. They can slice and dice facts and contemplate a future that is a continuation of the past. But they cannot explore the unknown and innovate into what has never been thought before.

TO PONDER

Maybe our fears about a future with "machine masters" is based on a lack of faith in mankind and its ability to evolve to the next stage—to become fit and survive.

For as long as mankind has been around, humans have been searching for ways to simplify their lives, reduce work, and increase comfort. This desire led to the invention of the knife to help man hunt, and the discovery of fire to keep man warm. It is this inherent need that has triggered the invention of electricity and telephone and caused the Industrial Revolution. The drive for more comfort, luxury, and security has led to practically every technological invention and scientific discovery from medicine to telecommunications, transportation, agriculture, and more.

Is the creation of artificial intelligence and robots any different? Or is it just the right set of capabilities and advancements we need for the times we live in and the era ahead?

Since 2000, the population in the U.S. has grown 2.4 times faster than jobs. However, jobs had grown 1.7 times faster than the population for over 50 years prior to that. Are the jobs going away or has our expectation of what jobs should be, what they should pay, and how they should be performed changed? Research offered in a KPCB and Mary Meeker report suggests that there is a clear disconnect between what is important to company managers versus the millennial generation. Managers think that "work pay" is close to 2 times more important, but in fact, millennials value "work being meaningful" 3 times more than managers. Additionally, millennials consider getting a sense of accomplishment from work to be 2 times more important than managers do. The same report indicates that freelancers now account for 53 million people (34% of U.S. work force)—a significant and growing portion of workers.

These trends suggest that perhaps people are ready for a new era. The era to focus on creativity, innovation, accomplishment, and meaningfulness of work. A time where humans are beginning to be less fascinated by being in control of tasks and mundane decisions, and more fascinated by making an impact.

Are the jobs and the nature of employment changing because of automation? Or have humans conceived and employed automation purposefully to change the nature of the work they no longer desire?

By 2020, the global market for pharmaceuticals will approach $1.4 trillion per year. By then, the inclusive cost of cancer treatment will reach $175 billion—a big business by all accounts. Think about all those involved in research, manufacturing and distribution of products, the doctors, the nurses, and the insurance clerks processing the claims and others—together representing millions of jobs.

So, if we cure cancer, jobs will be lost. Should we then not pursue this dream?

———

Maybe machines are the very thing we need to get to the next level of human evolution. They will augment our brain by processing more data and becoming more intelligent faster. Machines will free our minds and help us unleash our imagination. With our brains less taxed with the mundane and more focused on innovation perhaps we can evolve to experience a new state of collective consciousness. A state filled with promise.

We should build the machines, partner with them, and augment our intelligence. We should use artificial intelligence and the capabilities it offers as stimuli and make a quantum leap ahead—to the next human evolution.

This augmentation and partnership with technology and machines should not exclusively be an effort to gain efficiency. Augmenting your capabilities with machines should be a way to gain more speed, more computing power, and more knowledge. It should be the means to replace processing routine activities with more meaningful, innovative, and creative work.

Politics and religion may divide us, but data and machines could connect us and make us one world. A world where the boundaries of companies, services, and products are hard to distinguish. A world where constant innovation comes from all four corners of the earth. Where only the informed can truly evolve and abundance of data and ensuing insights will make the planet more knowledgeable and innovative.

As we get closer to a more advanced AI state, we must accept the eventuality of machines as our partners. It is up to us to define the roles and the nature of the relationship. It is up to us to go beyond the fear of being replaced and focus on leveraging our new augmented capabilities to advance humanity.

My "Two Minute Warning" for you is not about doom and gloom, not of machine mastery, and human slavery. *Warning*—exciting times are ahead. To survive and evolve, you must show up with all your imagination, stand-up with courage to change, buckle up to weather the tough ride ahead, and wise up by augmenting your capabilities.

There are over 86 billion neurons in the brain and all are ready to process information, ready to learn, and ready to issue commands, at any time. Believe in yourself and the rest of humanity. Don't fear the machines. The future is uncertain, align with it constantly. Appreciate the reality of change from job loss to augmented intelligence and start shaping your reality of tomorrow. Aspire to more, always. You deserve it.

Gain the caterpillar's edge. Evolve, evolve again, and thrive . . . in business, as an individual, as a society, and as the human race.

Dare to be a butterfly and lead a generation to its next evolution!

"Those who look only to the past or present are certain to miss the future . . . Change is the law of life."

**—John F. Kennedy,
U.S. President**

ACKNOWLEDGEMENTS

I have learned from many over the years: my clients, my colleagues—those who invested in my companies and entrepreneurs that I believed in and invested in—my students, my mentors, and my teachers. I am grateful to all for helping me shape my thoughts.

In writing this book the following individuals were particularly generous with their time and thoughtfulness.

Donald Beall

Former CEO and Chairman of Rockwell International and former board member for Procter & Gamble, Amoco, and Time Warner. *A true leader of complexity.*

Austin Beutner

Co-founder of Evercore Partners (the investment banking group with over $1.2 billion revenues in 2015); former First Deputy Mayor of Los Angeles; and past publisher and CEO of the Los Angeles Times and the San Diego Union-Tribune. *An expert in spotting opportunities and executing flawlessly.*

Adam Coates

An MIT Technology Review recognized under-35 innovator, a Stanford University researcher, and the Director of Baidu's (Google of China) Artificial Intelligence Lab in Silicon Valley. *An authentic visionary.*

Patrick Conway

The Chief Knowledge Officer (CKO) at U.S. Army Training and Doctrine Command (TRADOC), focusing on building the next generation of leaders in the U.S. Army. *An authority on team performance and mission critical challenges.*

Marty Cooper

A pioneer in the wireless communications industry; the visionary who conceived the first handheld mobile phone while heading up Motorola's communications systems; founder and investor in numerous technology companies.

Simply a genius.

Lynne Doughtie

The U.S. Chairman and Chief Executive Officer of KPMG—one of the world's leading professional services firms and the fastest growing Big Four firm in the U.S., employing close to 174,000 people globally with over $24 billion in revenues. *A compassionate and result oriented proven leader.*

Mark Goodburn

Chairman of KPMG's Global Advisory Executive Team with deep global experience in assisting Fortune 500 clients and serving on KPMG's Americas region board of directors as well as Middle East and India oversight boards.

An expert in global competitive dynamics.

J.P. Gownder

A Forrester Research principal analyst and VP; a thought leader in virtual and augmented reality, wearable computing, tablets, smart phones, and robotics.

A thought leader around drivers of innovation.

Arlene Harris

Known as the "First Lady of Wireless," the first woman inducted into the Wireless Hall of Fame; a serial entrepreneur, an inventor, and a successful investor. *An original entrepreneur and practical innovator.*

Steven Hill

Global Head of Innovation & Investments and a former Vice Chair at KPMG responsible for hundreds of millions of dollars of investments driving the firm's strategic growth initiatives.

An expert in spotting trends and large scale mobilization of change.

Chris Hoehn-Saric

Co-founder of Sterling Partners, a private equity firm with over $5 billion in assets under management; former CEO of multiple companies and an active board member. *A natural born company and market builder.*

Anne Hubert

Formerly a Senior Vice President at Viacom, Anne led Scratch, a creative consultancy. She also served as the Special Advisor for Millennial Engagement at Hillary for America (Hillary Clinton for President, 2016). *The expert on our next generation leaders, employees, and customers.*

Hans Imhof

Founder of EPE, of one of the largest uninterruptible power supplies manufacturers in the world, since sold to Group Schneider; started over a dozen companies and invested in many more. *A passionate and patient leader and investor.*

Robert Kleist

Founder and CEO of Printronix—which went from his garage to public markets—an inventor, an entrepreneur, an early stage investor, and a seasoned board member. *An expert in constantly mapping technology to unanticipated needs.*

Bryan Neider

A progressively successful corporate executive at Electronic Arts as CFO and COO for EA.com, CFO of Worldwide Studios, and Senior Vice President of Global Operations. *A veteran corporate leader in a hyper competitive market.*

Safi Qureshey

The co-founder and CEO of AST Research, Inc., a publicly traded personal computer manufacturer acquired by Samsung Electronics; a professor, an active investor and board member. *A skillful corporate and social entrepreneur.*

Ashwin Rangan

Former CIO at Rockwell International, Walmart.com, and Edwards Lifesciences; current Chief Innovation and Information Officer for ICANN (Internet Corporation for Assigned Names and Numbers), maintaining and coordinating Internet Protocol (IP) addresses and the Domain Name System.
A real strategist in the body of a technology leader.

Paul Slack

A Marine Corps brigadier general who was responsible for a $2.4 billion budget before he retired; an expert in large scale mission critical operations. *An expert in realizing the value of intelligence while facing life and death decisions.*

Mona Vernon

VP of Thomson Reuters Labs focusing on new data-driven innovations; a member of the Commonwealth of Massachusetts Big Data Committee; and winner of Boston's "50 on Fire".
An authority in use of analytics for innovation.

THANK YOU,

from the bottom of my heart.

INDEX

A

accountability, 128, 154

acknowledgment of allies, 64–68

adaptiveness, 86

Addair, George, 149

addiction, 3, 6, 10–11, 12, 13, 17, 18–19

    to stale and static processes, 7–10

Addiction Busters, 152

"Aha" moments, 26, 27, 29–30, 37–38, 61, 141, 156

AirBnb, 102, 125

Alexander the Great, 77

Alibaba, 69, 101

Alice in Wonderland (Carroll), 132–33

alignment with uncertainty, 30, 30, 104–20

allies, acknowledgment of, 64–68

Alphabet, 17, 47, 69, 127–28

Amazon, 53, 69, 101, 116–19, 124–25, 162

Amazon EC2, 118

Amoco, 138

analytical competition, 49, 55–56

analytics. See data analytics

Andreessen, Marc, 162

Android, 101, 127

Angelou, Maya, 98

apoptosis, 87

Apple, 10, 83–85, 101

application economy, 64

appreciate reality, 30, 30, 119, 128, 132

artificial intelligence, 158–64

Aspirational, as stage of analytics adoption, 65, 65

aspire for more, 30, 30, 132, 144

A.T. Kearney, 16

"at arms," 27

atomic power, 81, 114

AT&T, 123, 124

B

Experienced, as stage of analytics adoption, 65, 65

experimentation, 72, 75–76

F
Facebook, 10

failure, 6, 10–11, 13, 15, 75–76, 154

false reality, 116–20

financial services industry, 46, 102

Finley, Guy, 57

firemen, 108–9

Firestein, Stuart, 74

Fitbit, 52

Fitzgerald, Tom, 85

Five Forces framework, 38, 66

focus, 120–25

Ford, Henry, 73

Ford Motor Company, 53

Forrester Research, 47, 65–66

fortune makers, 107

fortune tellers, 107

Franklin, Benjamin, 58

freemium, 36

frictions, 148–49

G
Gallup, 69

Gandhi, Mahatma, 146

Gartner, 51

Gates, Bill, 13, 161

General Electric (GE), 37, 51

General Motors (GM), 84–85, 106, 111–12

generals and the soldiers, 26–29

Gerstner, Lou, 37

"get your head out of the boat," 147–48

Goldman Sachs, 70

Goodburn, Mark, 170

J

K

S

THE CATERPILLAR'S EDGE